Praise

"What a fabulous book! I wish I had this when I was dating years ago. Times have changed, and terms have changed but people have not. I also wish this was available for my daughters!"
--Marlene Gross-Ackeret

"The book is wonderful, and I wish I had known all this before I agreed to marry!"
--Gayle Shinder

"One of the things I really appreciate about this book is its practical approach. The book covers a wide range of red flags, including emotional manipulation, lack of communication, and controlling behavior, among others."
--Emily Thompson

"This book's emphasis is on empowering readers. It not only highlights the warning signs but also provides practical strategies and advice on how to address them. It feels like you have a trusted friend by your side, supporting you along the way."
--Olivia Johnson

RED FLAGS

Icks, Personality Quirks, or Warning Signs?
How to Know the Difference

Learn to spot narcissists, manipulators, liars, and the toxic, non-nurturing, unsupportive, self-absorbed. Rescue, protect, and heal yourself from emotional mistreatment and abuse

A CRASH COURSE IN RELATIONSHIP SELF DEFENSE

Diane Metcalf

FREE GIFT

To get the best experience possible from this book, I invite you to sign up for the free 8-week e-mail Survival Course and join The Toolbox for Healing.

Free 8-week Email Survival Course

Weekly topics, strategies, and homework for you to start moving forward from the effects of non-nurturing relationships, individuals with toxic traits, and Lemon Moms.

***

The Toolbox for Healing

Recover from Hurtful People and Relationships
Receive twice-monthly strategies right to your inbox!

***

Sign up for both here:

toolbox.dianemetcalf.com

Your Free Gift:
An Inner Child Guided Healing Meditation MP3

Dedication

For all of us.

*This book is dedicated to every individual
who has had the privilege
of being part of a relationship.*

*It is a reminder that we all have the power
to navigate the complexities
of love and connection with wisdom and discernment.*

Contents

"Staying vulnerable is a risk we must take
to experience connection."

—Brené Brown

FOREWORD

It is unfortunate that this book was not available decades ago. Red flags are hard to spot when they've become part of the fabric of your life. Diane and I share the same experiences of growing up in a dysfunctional home, with an absent father and an overwhelmed and mentally ill mother.

Because human beings are biologically wired for connectedness, it is important to develop the ability to identify behaviors and traits that can serve as warning signs of an unhealthy relationship- whether it be a romantic, friendship, family, or workplace relationship. Sometimes our early life experiences disable our ability to recognize those warning bells and red flags.

Diane provides a validating framework for us to gain a deeper understanding of those warning signs and empowers us to trust our inner voice and take action when something feels "off."

She creates a safe haven for the reader to explore these concepts and has compassionately alerted the reader to potentially triggering materials. Diane explains the cues, attitudes and behaviors that can alert us to potentially damaging relationships, in contrast to harmless quirks and unique mannerisms. We are sensitively led through the spectrum of individual differences, recognizing the flags, identifying abuse and potential danger, identifying the symptoms of distress and trauma, codependency, self-care, and the ongoing process of healing.

Diane's well researched content, combined with her playful humor and frank personal experiences create the supportive environment required for us to gain awareness, stand in our power, and set the personal boundaries required to have the satisfying and fulfilling relationships that we all deserve.

As a mental health therapist, I am looking forward to sharing this book with my own clients. We all can gain insight and awareness from this valuable resource, to facilitate self-healing and love.

Rev. Hollie Ann Brooks, Licensed Mental Health Counselor, LMHC

Certified Shamanic Healer and Practitioner (Pachakuti Mesa Tradition-PMT)
Angelic Liquid Light Practitioner
Certified Keith's Cacao Facilitator (Plant Medicine)
Reiki Master
Sound Healing
Ordained Minister, Order of Melchizedek
Headway- https://headway.co/providers/hollie-brooks
Heal Me- https://heal.me/practitioner/hollie-brooks

PREFACE

Understanding relationship **red flags** is like having a secret superpower that can help us navigate relationships. These little warning signs or behaviors sometimes pop up, waving their arms, saying, "Hey, pay attention! There might be trouble ahead!" Knowing what these signs look like can help us make more informed decisions about any relationship with family, friends, coworkers, or romantic partners.

Let's talk about dating. Ah, the thrill of meeting someone new and exciting! But before we get too carried away, let's remember to keep our eyes and ears open for potential warning signs. Our well-being matters, and by understanding and recognizing relationship warning signs, we can better protect ourselves from the potential emotional, physical, or psychological harm that may arise. It's like putting on a suit of armor, but instead of metal, it's *made of knowledge and self-awareness*. These warning signs can help us steer clear of anyone who may be emotionally unavailable, abusive, or just plain incompatible with our principles. This awareness can protect us from frustration, dissatisfaction, and even mistreatment.

And here's the best part: developing the skills to identify these signs early can *help us avoid* potentially harmful relationships altogether! It's like having a built-in radar that guides us away from trouble and towards healthier connections. Plus, it helps us set boundaries and manage our expectations, leading to more positive encounters.

I hope you join me on this transformative expedition as we delve into the intricate tapestry of human interactions and the delicate balance between connection and self-preservation. Together, we will navigate the sometimes-hazardous realm of relationships, armed with information that can guide us toward more fulfilling relationships.

We will uncover the hidden patterns and subconscious biases that can lead us astray and we'll empower ourselves to make informed choices that align with our true desires and values. This journey of self-discovery will illuminate the path toward healthier relationships and serve as a testament to the resilience of the human spirit and its capacity for growth and transformation. So, get ready to embark on an odyssey of awareness, self-discovery, and empowerment as we leave past missteps behind and embrace a future filled with love, authenticity, fulfillment, and a constant feeling of safety and security.

PART 1:
ICKS, QUIRKS, OR WARNING SIGNS?

Content Warning:

This section contains frank discussions of relationship red flags, mental health challenges, and other sensitive topics including neglect and abuse. Please be aware that reading about these issues may be difficult for some readers.

Reader discretion is advised.

INTRODUCTION

This book serves as a tribute to the power of awareness.

In a world where love and companionship are highly valued and sought, it becomes necessary to navigate our relationships cautiously. For too many of us, the path to relationship happiness has been riddled with obstacles and painful experiences.

Red flags are warning signs or behaviors that may indicate potential problems or issues in any relationship. The ability to recognize these signs can help us make more informed choices and decisions about our relationships, including those with family, friends, coworkers, and romantic partners.

As a young, single person years ago, the concept of **red flags** was unknown to me. I was repeatedly drawn to partners who were not good for me, and I felt trapped in a cycle of heartache and disappointment. Although my intuition often warned me that something was amiss, I often ignored or denied my instincts. Only hindsight revealed the significance of those feelings and the potential for a different outcome had I heeded them. So, if you're dating, your awareness of potential **red flags** may help you avoid becoming involved with someone who may be incompatible with your values and goals, and save you from heartbreak, disappointment, and even potential harm.

Understanding the warning signs can enhance your relationships with family members, friends, and colleagues too. By recognizing potentially harmful patterns of interaction or behavior, you can take proactive measures to avoid toxic dynamics and nurture positive connections with those who share your values and aspirations.

In this book, I delve into concepts of personality quirks and idiosyncrasies, relationship dynamics, and the definitions and differences in what is meant by terms like toxicity, dysfunction, mental health, and abuse. You'll learn how to protect yourself from unhealthy relationships. By honing your ability to discern the warning signs, set boundaries, and manage expectations, you may enjoy more satisfying relationship experiences!

My hope is to empower you in making informed decisions and cultivating nourishing relationships for your well-being and enjoyment.

I wish you the best in life, love, and happiness!

Diane

Chapter One
UNDERSTANDING THE DISTINCTION: ICKS AND PERSONALITY QUIRKS

Welcome to the wild and wonderful world of relationship **red flags**! Now, before we dive into this chapter, let's take a moment to acknowledge something important: we're all human, and that means we all have our quirks and imperfections. Trust me, I've got my fair share too! So, let's approach this topic with a healthy dose of self-compassion, and even a little humor, OK?

Relationship **red flags** are like neon signs, flashing warnings that something might not be quite right. They're the little indicators that make us pause and think, "Hmm, maybe I should proceed with caution here." But fear not, my friend, because recognizing them is not about pointing fingers or passing judgment. *It's about empowering ourselves to make better choices and build more fulfilling relationships.*

Think of it as a crash course in relationship self-defense. By learning to spot the warning signs, we may gain a little extra protection.

This book isn't about shaming or blaming anyone. *It's about arming ourselves with knowledge and awareness.* So, grab your detective hat and magnifying glass because we're about to embark on a journey of discovery. We'll explore the subtle cues that can help us navigate relationships with a little more confidence and a lot less drama.

But remember, dear reader, *we're all a work in progress*. As we delve in, let's do so *with a healthy dose of self-reflection.* After all, it's not just about spotting the signs in others; it's about recognizing them in ourselves too. Let's embrace our imperfections, laugh at our own quirks, and actively work on making any necessary changes as we embark on this adventure of learning, growth and building healthier relationships.

So, buckle up and get ready for insights, anecdotes, and maybe even a few facepalms. Because when it comes to relationship **red flags**, knowledge truly is power. Let's dive in!

UNDERSTANDING THE SPECTRUM OF "DIFFERENT"

Have you ever met someone who seemed a bit "different" or maybe had some unique personality traits? Sometimes, it can be challenging to figure out if those traits are harmless or if they could potentially be warning signs. Yet, distinguishing between icks, harmless eccentricities, and genuine red flags is critical for our personal safety. By learning how to identify narcissists, manipulators, liars, and others who display self-centeredness and lack empathy, you can make informed decisions and take the necessary action to protect, rescue, and heal yourself from the abuse you may encounter.

In our interactions, it's a good idea to develop an ability to identify behaviors and traits that could indicate danger by learning to differentiate between harmless idiosyncrasies and undisputable warning signs.

BEYOND BUZZWORDS: FEELING THE ICK

You have probably heard of THE ICK. You've definitely *felt* the ick at some point in your life. The "ick" factor refers to a moment when something happens or is revealed about a person that is so profoundly disgusting or off-putting that it causes you to cringe. Feeling "the ick" is like a sudden wave of disgust that washes over you, causing you to recoil and lose the feelings you once felt for that person. The ick is triggered by something seemingly insignificant, yet it feels *extremely* significant, and resonates within your very core. It's a gut instinct that tells you that this person is not right for you, a realization that echoes so deeply that it shakes the foundation of your connection with them.

UNDERSTANDING HARMLESS PERSONALITY QUIRKS: A BALANCED PERSPECTIVE

It's important to remember that not every behavior that seems strange or uncomfortable is a cause for concern. To differentiate between icks, harmless quirks, and true warning signs, it's crucial to consider the following:

Context and cultural differences: Certain behaviors may be influenced by cultural norms or personal backgrounds. What may appear peculiar to you could be perfectly acceptable within someone else's cultural context. For example, in many Western cultures, people tend to value and keep a certain distance between themselves and others during conversations or interactions. However, in some Middle Eastern or Latin American cultures, it is common for people to stand closer to each other and have more physical contact during conversations. So, what may seem like invading personal space in one culture is actually a sign of friendliness and engagement in another.

Individual uniqueness: Each person has their own idiosyncrasies and peculiarities that make them unique. While some behaviors may seem strange, they do not necessarily pose a threat to your well-being.

Personality quirks and *non-threatening eccentricities* are those little treasures that make a person interesting. They're the special traits that add depth and character to someone's personality. These quirks can be harmless and even endearing, without any negative impact on others. For example, imagine someone who always arranges their books on their bookshelf in a specific order, by color or size. It may seem peculiar to some, but it's just a fun and harmless way for them to express their individuality. So, embrace those quirks and celebrate what makes each person special!

"I was on a date with someone I had been seeing for a few weeks. We were having a great time, laughing and enjoying each other's company. But then, out of nowhere, they made a derogatory comment about a group of people. It was so shocking and offensive that I immediately felt the ick. A feeling of disgust came over me, and I couldn't shake it. From that moment on, I knew that this person's values and beliefs were not aligned with mine, and it was a clear red flag for me to end the relationship." —
Anonymous

A CRUCIAL SKILL FOR DATING: NAVIGATING THE MAZE OF SOCIAL MEDIA

Dating advice can be elaborate, complex, and challenging to decipher, no matter how many Taylor Swift albums you've analyzed. With so much advice out there, it can be tough to figure out the difference between icks, personality quirks, and red flags. But understanding the difference between them is a priceless skill when deciding whether someone is truly worth your time or not.

I think it's necessary to reevaluate the buzzwords that dominate social media and discussions about relationships, because when it comes to identifying warning signs and red flags, I've seen some real doozies. For example, if someone does not like pizza, and you do, it is *not* a red flag. It might bother you that someone you're interested in doesn't like the things that you do, but it's not a warning sign of potential danger. And if someone has no memory of a conversation because they *genuinely do not remember* it, that is *not* an example of gaslighting. We'll talk more about gaslighting in later chapters, but for now, know that gaslighting is a form of *intentional* psychological manipulation, an act of influencing or controlling someone deceptively. A gaslighter denies or distorts the truth, *to intentionally* cause someone to doubt themselves, and feel confused, anxious, and powerless. Genuine gaslighting *is* a red flag. Do you see the difference?

With the proliferation of bad dating and relationship advice out there, it's key to stay informed through multiple venues and to consider the *context* behind the *content*. By that, I mean knowing who created the content you consume. What are their qualifications? Are they pretending to be someone or something they're not? This consideration also applies to questioning the broader narratives presented by any platform's algorithms. Algorithms are complex mathematical formulas that social media platforms use to decide what content to show you. They analyze your preferences and engagement levels to decide which posts, ads, and recommendations you are most likely to find interesting. The goal is to enhance your experience by showing content to you that you are more likely to engage with, thereby increasing your level of satisfaction and platform usage.

Sometimes algorithms promote trending ideas like "all men suck" or push a type of "dump-them" mentality touted as empowerment or "feminism." Beware that a platform's algorithm is *supposed* to show you more of what you've already searched for or clicked on, and it prioritizes your content based on *showing you more of the same.* That may do the opposite of what you intended; it may work to defeat your goal. You may be shown more of what's hurtful about relationships, keeping you stuck, preventing you from moving forward. Just be aware, is all I'm saying.

Chapter Two
DECODING THE METAPHOR: UNMASKING THE FLAGS

Do you know someone who consistently brings conflict and stress into your life? You might think of them as challenging, difficult, or even toxic.

UNDERSTANDING THE DIFFERENCE: CHALLENGING VS. TOXIC

There's a difference in what the terms challenging, difficult, and toxic mean. A "*difficult*" person exhibits challenging or demanding behaviors, but they do not necessarily have harmful intentions or engage in manipulative tactics. They likely have personal struggles that make it difficult for them to interact positively with others, which may be permanent or temporary.

On the other hand, a "*toxic*" person consistently engages in *manipulative, controlling, or abusive* behaviors that *harm others*. They intentionally look to undermine or emotionally, mentally, or even physically hurt others. Personally, I don't like the term "toxic person." I believe it is more helpful to focus on *specific behaviors* or *dynamics* that cause harm or distress rather than to label a person as "toxic."

Toxic traits can include manipulative behavior, lack of empathy, constant criticism, a tendency to exert control over others, gaslighting, seeking constant reassurance, blaming others, and evading responsibility. It is important to note that these traits can vary from person to person, and not all people with toxic behavior will have all these traits (WebMD).

Understand the difference between difficult people and those with toxic traits so you can take proper action to protect yourself.

IDENTIFYING SIGNS OF TOXICITY: A NECESSARY SKILL

A "red flag" is a term that's often used to describe warning signs or indicators of potential problems or issues. In relationships, red flags refer to behaviors or behavior patterns that may indicate the need for a closer look because they may become more serious interpersonal problems. It's important to note that red flags *are not definitive proof of a problem but **are signals that deserve further attention*** or investigation. (Gould, 2023)

A red flag is a cautionary signal that pops up, indicating something that could be a potential issue or a challenge that might arise later. These red flags come in various forms, such as someone excessively talking about themselves, avoiding difficult conversations, gossiping about their ex, or even withholding affection. They may manifest as negative behaviors, verbal or physical cues, or subtle hints of a personality trait that needs closer examination. Red flags could develop into hurtful or harmful behaviors if not recognized early.

So, let's explore the significance of recognizing people with toxic traits as an essential step in safeguarding ourselves.

When identifying people with toxic traits, we must recognize the *signs that highlight the harmful behavior.* ***These signs help us differentiate between someone going through life's everyday difficulties and someone consistently showing traits of "toxicity."*** Individuals with toxic traits have a talent for creating negativity and upset, causing emotional and sometimes physical pain to those around them.

In the field of mental health, the term "disorder" is used to describe ***a pattern of thoughts, feelings, or behaviors*** that significantly differ from what is considered "typical" or healthy. The classification of certain behaviors as "disorders" is *decided by professionals* like psychologists and psychiatrists, based on extensive research, clinical observations, and diagnostic criteria.

Toxicity is not classified as a mental "disorder." Still, it is possible that underlying mental health challenges **can contribute** to someone's toxic behavior.

Allow me to repeat: **Toxicity is not a mental disorder**. The person in question may have underlying mental health struggles contributing to their toxic behavior. Often, such individuals are dealing with their own stresses and traumas, which they express in ways that upset or harm others.

---

*It is important to clarify **that the term "toxic person" refers to a person's way of thinking and behaving.** It is imperative to consider the context and potential impact of using this label and to use it with caution and empathy. Labeling someone as "toxic" can be hurtful and will not contribute to a productive conversation or resolution.*

The following list includes several critical toxic traits to be aware of when deciding whether to pursue any relationship.

IDENTIFYING TOXIC BEHAVIOR: KEY INDICATORS

To ensure you are involved in a safe and fulfilling relationship, it is crucial to be aware of and address any warning signs early. The following list highlights some warning signs of people with toxic traits.

Each point stands for an attitude or behavior that could negatively affect your well-being:

Addiction/abuses substances: People can find themselves medically addicted to a variety of substances and behaviors. These can include but are not limited to alcohol, nicotine (tobacco), illegal drugs like cocaine, heroin, and methamphetamines, prescription drugs such as opioids, benzodiazepines, and stimulants, gambling, food, sex, and even internet or video games. It's important to note that addiction is a *severe medical condition* characterized by compulsive use despite harmful consequences, and it often involves changes in the brain's functioning.

Addiction becomes incredibly destructive when it consistently harms not only the addicted individual but those around them, and manifests in several ways such as verbal abuse (yelling, name-calling), theft, dishonesty, neglect, and evasion of responsibility (Dumain, T. 2022).

If you are affected by someone's addiction, it's essential to find support through various resources such as support groups, counseling services, community centers, and addiction treatment centers. These places often provide a safe and understanding environment where individuals can share their experiences, receive guidance, and connect with others who are going through similar situations. Additionally, online forums and social media groups dedicated to addiction recovery can be valuable sources of support and information. In the United States, contact SAMHSA, the Substance Abuse and Mental Health Services Administration- https://www.findtreatment.gov. In Europe, contact the European Federation of Addiction Societies- https://www.eufas.net/.

Aggression or violent behavior: Frequent angry displays, physical aggression, or threats toward others can be warning signs of potential danger. Aggressive or violent behavior can show the potential for harm. When someone displays aggressive or violent behavior, *it suggests that they have difficulty controlling their emotions or impulses,* which can lead to harmful actions towards you or others. Examples of aggressive, angry, or violent behavior include verbal threats or insults, intimidation tactics, property damage, and acts of violence towards themselves or others, including physical fights, assault, and homicide. Several factors, including underlying mental health issues, past trauma, substance abuse, or a combination thereof, can influence aggressive or violent behavior.

Earlier instances of physical aggression or violence, especially if they were unprovoked or severe, may also indicate a potential for future danger. Research in the field of psychology has shown that **individuals with a history of aggression or violence are more likely to engage in similar behaviors in the future.** Some notable researchers in this field include Dr. Robert Hare, who has extensively studied psychopathy and its association with aggression, and Dr. James Gilligan, who has focused on the relationship between violence and mental health challenges. Additionally, studies published in journals such as the Journal of Abnormal Psychology, Journal of Consulting and Clinical Psychology, and Journal of Forensic Psychology supply valuable insights into the link between aggression, violence, and potential danger.

If you're interested in learning more, I recommend exploring trustworthy sources such as academic journals, textbooks, or websites of reputable mental health organizations. These resources can provide more in-depth information and specific references to support your understanding of aggressive or violent behavior as red flags.

Attention seeks: Whether it's constant phone calls, text messages, or unannounced visits, attention-seeking individuals require much of your time and emotional support. They need almost constant validation, but they will rarely reciprocate that support to you. There is an elevated level of self-interest here, and this behavior is often associated with **narcissistic personality disorder (NPD).**

Blames: It is a red flag when someone makes a mistake or a poor choice and blames others for the consequences. It suggests a lack of accountability and an unwillingness to take responsibility for one's actions. Blaming an ex for a past relationship breakdown may show an inability to take responsibility for their contributions within the broken relationship.

Blaming suggests an unwillingness to learn from mistakes or work on personal growth, *which can lead to a cycle of repeating the same patterns* in future relationships. Blaming, rather than engaging in **self-reflection and introspection**, may also show a lack of empathy and understanding towards others, a reluctance to understand other viewpoints, or a disregard for the effects of their actions on others.

Blaming can have negative consequences in personal relationships, work environments, and other areas where accountability and responsibility are important. Blaming is always a red flag.

Controls others or has manipulative tendencies: A lack of trust and respect in a relationship can manifest as a tendency to control others. If someone tries to control your actions and decisions or who you spend time with, it could be a sign of a toxic relationship. Watch for individuals who consistently try to control or influence your thoughts, emotions, or actions.

Just because someone desires you does not mean they value you.

Controllers and manipulators often employ cunning tactics to exploit or dominate others for their own gain. They resort to lying or distorting the truth, exaggerating, or omitting information to control your actions or opinions of them. Controllers and manipulators go to great lengths to achieve their goals, even when they know it will hurt others.

Controlling and manipulative behavior restricts the freedom and autonomy of another person, can lead to power imbalances within a relationship, and pose a risk to the other's well-being. Healthy relationships are built on trust, equality, and mutual respect. When a person tries to control or manipulate another's actions, decisions, or social interactions, it can be a warning sign of coercive control and potential control-issues in the relationship.

Criticizes, belittles, name-calls, claims that no one else would want or love you: Critiquing and belittling, calling you crazy, stupid, fat, unattractive, or claiming that no one else would want or love you is a hurtful method of manipulation and control, and **emotionally abusive behavior**. Over time, hearing these statements may erode your self-esteem or cause you to feel trapped and isolated.

"I once had a teammate who always seemed to bring negativity into the workplace. He would gossip about others, spread rumors, and it felt like a toxic environment. Whenever he was around, you could feel the tension in the air. It became clear that he had toxic traits when he started to belittle others to make them feel inferior. Recognizing these traits allowed us to distance ourselves from him and create a healthier and more positive work environment." —Anonymous

Defensive: Defensiveness can be a sign of toxicity because it often shows a lack of openness or a refusal to take responsibility for one's actions. When someone is defensive, they may become overly protective of their image and unwilling to admit mistakes, creating a hostile, unhealthy environment where concerns and conflicts are not addressed. In a healthy relationship, both parties feel comfortable and safe, expressing their thoughts and feelings without fear of judgment or retaliation.

Demands to know your whereabouts or bombards you with calls, emails, and texts: Continually needing to know your whereabouts or bombarding you with calls, emails, and texts throughout the day shows a possible lack of trust, disrespect for your personal boundaries, or a high degree of insecurity. It can also signify jealousy, a desire to control, and other coercive behaviors. All red flags.

Desires to rush into a relationship quickly: Pushing you into a committed relationship status can be a sign of emotional immaturity, insecurity, low self-esteem, jealousy, or a desire for control. It may suggest that the person is not taking the time to truly get to know you and set up a solid foundation for the relationship, which can lead to future issues with communication, trust, managing expectations and connecting emotionally.

Dishonesty: Honesty and trust are vital for a relationship to last. Open, honest communication is necessary for building trust and keeping a strong bond. Dishonesty undermines trust, and it can lead to feelings of betrayal and damage the relationship's foundation. Dishonest individuals have a habit of lying, fabricating stories or manipulating facts to serve their own agenda. If someone lies or withholds valuable information, it may show a lack of trustworthiness. Consistent patterns of deceitfulness are red flags.

Displays anger or rage towards you but not others: Showing angry feelings towards you but keeping composure around others suggests that this individual may have anger management issues. This behavior can be emotionally and mentally draining because of constant feelings of being on edge, fearful, or "walking on eggshells," and trying to keep them calm and stable. It raises concerns about how they may treat people when behind closed doors; they may be hiding their true nature from those outside of their relationships.

Disregards your consent: Any form of non-consensual behavior, whether it's physical, emotional, or sexual, is a major red flag and should never be ignored. Disregarding your consent shows a lack of respect for your personal boundaries, autonomy, and well-being. Consent is a fundamental aspect of healthy relationships, and when someone consistently disregards or violates your consent, it signals manipulative, abusive behavior.

Emotionally unavailable: Emotional support and intimacy are necessary for a fulfilling connection. A lack of emotional openness or willingness to connect on a deeper level can lead to difficulty building and keeping a healthy relationship, resulting in feelings of neglect, frustration, and dissatisfaction with the relationship.

Excludes: When someone withholds affection and attention, shuts us out, or makes us feel like outsiders, it can be a sign that they are trying to control or manipulate us. This behavior can be damaging to our self-esteem, emotional health, and overall well-being. Exclusion can be a form of emotional manipulation and is a red flag.

Ghosts: Abruptly ending all communication and contact with someone, typically in a romantic or social relationship, without any explanation or warning is called ghosting. It is often done by ignoring messages and calls, and effectively disappearing. Ghosting violates trust and shows disrespect for our feelings. When someone ghosts us, it sends the message that they believe our feelings are irrelevant and not worth even a brief explanation or goodbye. Not only does it leave us feeling angry or betrayed, but it can also negatively affect our sense of self-worth.

From a psychological standpoint, ghosting can leave lasting emotional scars, especially when combined with pre-existing low self-esteem from earlier abandonment experiences.

History of emotionally or physically abusing others: A history of physically or emotionally abusing others shows a lack of respect and a tendency to control others. It may suggest potential harm towards others through the use of coercive control.

High drama: Have you ever noticed that some individuals are constantly surrounded by drama? This is not a coincidence. People with toxic traits thrive in chaotic situations that fuel emotions and provoke conflicts. These individuals derive pleasure from "stirring the pot," as one therapist so aptly described it. They are not interested in doing the necessary work to keep stable and healthy relationships, instead, they prefer conflict and chaos.

Ignores boundaries: A clear sign of someone's toxicity is a disregard for personal boundaries. Despite your many attempts to communicate your needs, they will persistently disrespect, break, and overstep your boundaries. Healthy relationships respect boundaries, which people with toxic traits are incapable of or unwilling to do.

Impulsive/reckless: Impulsivity and recklessness suggest a lack of self-discipline and an inability to think about the potential outcomes of one's actions, resulting in behaviors that potentially jeopardize the safety and well-being of oneself and others. Engaging in impulsive or reckless actions without considering the consequences may indicate a lack of self-restraint or a disregard for personal safety.

Inconsistent: If someone's actions and words don't align, it could be a warning sign. People with toxic traits are known to display erratic behavior and often do not follow through on their commitments or promises. Their actions can be unpredictable, making it challenging to set up *a stable and reliable relationship* with them. One moment, they may be supportive, but the next, they may turn on you.

For example, if someone claims to be looking for a committed relationship but regularly avoids making plans or shows a lack of interest in knowing you better, that's inconsistency. Additionally, if someone often cancels plans or changes their mind about their feelings towards you, it may show a lack of stability or reliability. Paying attention to these discrepancies is essential as they could point to future issues.

Indifferent: A lack of interest, concern, or emotion towards someone or something is a state of not caring, apathy, or indifference. It signifies a lack of emotional investment or regard for an individual's emotions and needs, resulting in limited communication, emotional detachment, and an overall feeling of disengagement. It is essential to address any indifference early because its presence makes a healthy and fulfilling relationship nearly impossible.

Incompatible: Significant differences in values, goals, or lifestyles can lead to conflicts and misunderstandings. When two people have fundamentally different beliefs, aspirations, or ways of living, finding common ground and building a solid foundation for a healthy and fulfilling relationship can be challenging. Sharing similar values, goals, and lifestyles helps to ensure long-term compatibility.

Jealous: Jealousy often stems from feelings of insecurity, fear, or a lack of trust. When someone is jealous, it can lead to controlling behaviors, possessiveness, and a constant need for reassurance. This can create an unhealthy dynamic where one person feels suffocated or restricted in their personal freedom, leading to dissatisfaction with the relationship. It's important to address jealousy early because it can greatly impact the trust and emotional well-being of both individuals involved.

Lack of apology: When someone consistently refuses to apologize for their actions, it shows a lack of accountability and no respect for your feelings. Consistently withholding apologies may create a cycle of hurt and frustration, where you're left feeling invalidated and unheard. It can indicate a power imbalance within the relationship, where action is taken by one without considering the impact it will have on the other. If you constantly wait for an apology that never comes it may indicate a dynamic that deserves a closer look.

Be with someone who cares why you've been quiet all day, not with someone who gets angry because you're acting differently.

Lack of communication/poor communication: Effective communication is crucial for a healthy and successful relationship. If someone consistently avoids open and honest conversations or often dismisses your feelings or concerns, it's time to examine this more closely.

Poor communication can lead to misunderstandings, frustration, and a lack of emotional connection. It makes it difficult to resolve conflicts and address issues. If you're facing difficulties with communication in your relationship, express your concerns to see if there is willingness to work together to find a resolution. Effective communication skills are essential for building trust, understanding each other's needs and desires, and keeping a strong emotional bond.

Lack of respect: Respect is a fundamental aspect of any healthy relationship. When someone consistently shows a lack of respect, or contempt, it can indicate a lack of empathy, understanding, and consideration. A lack of respect can lead to a toxic, unhealthy dynamic, leaving you feeling devalued or mistreated. Establishing mutual respect and treating each other with kindness and dignity is essential to building a solid and fulfilling relationship.

You can gauge the level of respect someone has for others by watching their behavior and actions. Pay attention to how they communicate and interact with waitstaff, neighbors, strangers, friends, and family members. Look for signs of empathy, kindness, and consideration towards others. Additionally, notice if they listen actively, show genuine interest in others' perspectives, and treat everyone with dignity. It's important to remember that respect is not just about how someone treats you, but also how they treat others. Disrespect or contempt towards others will eventually extend to partners as well.

Monopolizes your time or discourages you from spending time with friends or family: These actions can be signs of controlling behavior, excessive neediness, or a lack of respect for your independence and personal relationships. They may also indicate insecurity or jealousy.

Poor relationships with friends or family: Healthy relationships are important to overall well-being. When someone consistently struggles to keep positive and fulfilling connections with the people closest to them, it may suggest underlying troubles such as poor communication skills, difficulty forming and keeping emotional bonds, or inability to resolve conflicts. Recognizing this pattern can signal that deeper emotional or interpersonal struggles may need to be addressed.

Preoccupation with violence or harm: While it is important in certain professions to be prepared for dangerous situations, an excessive fixation on violence or harm may suggest a potential for an abuse of power or a lack of self-control. It is crucial to gather more information and assess the context of this behavior before making any conclusions. An excessive preoccupation with violence, harm, or weapons, especially when combined with a fascination for past violent acts, deserves a closer look.

Pressures you to give up things you enjoy: When someone pressures you to give up personal things such as hobbies, activities, an education, friends, career goals, or your job, it shows a lack of respect for your individuality, independence, and personal growth. This behavior may also indicate feelings of jealousy, insecurity, or a need for control.

Rationalizes their behavior: Making excuses or justifications for their actions can show a lack of accountability or an unwillingness to take responsibility for their behavior, a sign of potential manipulative or deceptive tendencies.

Refuses to compromise: Compromise is an essential aspect of healthy relationships because it allows both parties to have their needs and desires met. When someone consistently refuses to compromise, it may indicate a lack of willingness to work together and find common ground, leading to resentment, conflict, and an imbalance of power in the relationship.

Secretive: An overly private or guarded individual may feel a lack of trust and discomfort with being candid. When someone is secretive, it can create a sense of unease, making it challenging to build a strong and healthy connection. Openness and honesty are essential for building trust and fostering a strong bond.

I once had a partner who adamantly refused to discuss their past, saying 'the past is in the past. What difference does it make now?' I found it quite peculiar, it raised some concerns, and the warning bells were sounding. Despite my instincts telling me otherwise, I adopted their perspective and disregarded my gut feelings. Unfortunately, it wasn't until we were deeply involved that I stumbled upon the hidden truths they were concealing. I seriously wished I'd heeded the warnings.

Self-centered: Pay attention to individuals who show excessive self-absorption and regularly prioritize their needs and desires over those of others. Such behavior can indicate a lack of consideration and compassion. These individuals may exhibit attention-seeking behavior and may be unwilling to compromise or make sacrifices. Self-centeredness can create feelings of imbalance and resentment within a relationship, leading to further dissatisfaction with the relationship. It is essential to consider each other's perspectives and needs to have a lasting relationship.

Showers you with compliments and it feels too good to be true: Although it feels great to be shown so much affection and attention, constantly receiving praise, compliments, or gifts from someone can be a sign of "**love bombing,**" a type of manipulation and exploitation.

Love-bombing involves showering someone with excessive affection, attention, and compliments to create a quick, intense, and sometimes overwhelming emotional bond. It often happens in the early stages of a romantic relationship, where the love-bomber constantly dotes on you and makes grand gestures of affection. It can also occur in other types of relationships, both new and established. Although it may not seem so, love-bombing can be incredibly deceptive and emotionally damaging. Excessive attention and affection can make anyone feel incredibly special but it is crucial to understand that this behavior is not genuine or sustainable. The love-bomber is not actually interested in your well-being or happiness; instead, they use these manipulative tactics to gain control and power over you.

Over time, the love-bomber's intentions will become clear. Once they have gained your trust and emotional dependence, they may begin to exert control by manipulating your emotions and isolating you from friends and family, leading to a toxic relationship where you feel alone, trapped, without outside support, and unable to get out.

Takes advantage of your finances: When someone uses your money for their personal benefit or accumulates debt on your credit cards, it shows a lack of respect for your financial boundaries. This behavior can create a power imbalance in the relationship, leading to economic instability due to their disregard for the impact their choices have on your financial well-being.

Talks badly about others: A negative and judgmental attitude toward others can indicate a lack of empathy and compassion, as they are willing to speak without considering the impact of their words. It could also indicate insecurity or a need to boost their own self-esteem by putting others down. Additionally, it may suggest a tendency towards gossip and drama; they may enjoy stirring up conflict by spreading untrue, inaccurate, and harmful information.

Triangulates: This term describes a situation where one person manipulates the communication between two other individuals. This person controls the narrative and decides how much and what type of exchange the other two individuals have with each other.

An example could be if a person says something untrue about one family member to another, intentionally generating rivalry by creating tension and confusion between the two. If someone controls the storyline or the type of communication that you have in another relationship, recognize it as a warning sign.

Trust issues: A lack of trust may indicate unhealed past traumas or unresolved difficulties, affecting one's ability to form healthy and meaningful relationships. Trust issues can lead to difficulties in communication and emotional intimacy.

Virtue signaling: This is a type of not-so-humble bragging about one's morals and values. Examples could include statements like "I'm a generous person," "I'm extremely open-minded," or "I'm very patient." It is essential to note that their words may not align with their actions. Most people with admirable character and integrity *do not* feel a need to announce or advertise it; they live it, and others notice. If someone needs to convince others of their positive qualities, it may be a red flag.

In the next chapter we'll shift our focus towards the impact of mental health and explore how the mental well-being of both ourselves and others affects our relationships.

Chapter Three
MENTAL HEALTH CHALLENGES IN RELATIONSHIPS

While reflecting on my own mental health challenges with depression, I've come to understand that mental health is the cornerstone of well-being; it allows us and our communities ***to function optimally.***

Mental health and emotional well-being are personal and complex topics requiring sensitivity and understanding. We all have highs and lows, and the signs we're talking about here can certainly be a part of life as we know it. But here's the thing: if they persist or start interfering with day-to-day life, it might be more than going through a "rough patch." If someone displays any of the mental health warning signs, it does not necessarily mean that there is a mental health issue, but *it is* crucial to acknowledge that "recognizing the signs" is a first step toward understanding and addressing potential mental health concerns.

Mental health challenges can show themselves in a variety of ways, not always easily identifiable, even for mental health professionals. That being said, it's a good idea to reach out to mental health experts if you have questions.

Mental health challenges are often unseen but deeply felt. Psychological difficulties and neurological issues can generate unwelcome changes in someone's emotions, thought processes, and behavior. Sometimes, all three can be affected at once. Variations in someone's mental well-being can profoundly affect their relationships, and make it challenging to function in social, work and family settings.

"I had a close friend who was constantly worried about the future and started isolating herself from social activities. One day, I decided to have a heart-to-heart with her and expressed my concern. I encouraged her to seek professional help and offered to go with her to her therapy sessions. Over time, she began to manage her symptoms and it was inspiring to witness her healing journey." —Anonymous

BEHIND THE LABEL: EXPLORING THE DEFINITION OF DISORDER

As previously mentioned, the term "disorder" is used to describe a pattern of thoughts, feelings, or behaviors that significantly deviate from what is considered "typical" or healthy. It is important to note that the classification of certain behaviors as disorders is decided by professionals in the field, such as psychologists and psychiatrists, based on extensive research, clinical observations, and diagnostic criteria outlined in widely accepted manuals like the Diagnostic and Statistical Manual of Mental Disorders (DSM-5). These professionals use their expertise and knowledge to assess and diagnose individuals, considering several factors such as the impact of these behaviors on daily functioning and overall well-being.

It is crucial to understand that the labeling of behaviors as "disorders" *is not a judgment*, but rather *a way to categorize and understand the complexities of mental health.*

Now let's explore the intricacies of the four mental health warning sign categories: emotional, behavioral, cognitive, and relational. By delving into each of them, we can gain a deeper understanding of their significance and how they relate to one's well-being.

WARNING SIGNS CONCERNING EMOTIONAL WELL-BEING

By acknowledging the warning signs related to one's emotional well-being, we *can gain insight into their overall well-being*, and navigate our relationship with greater clarity.

These signs are *not to be confused with a diagnosis or used as diagnostic criteria.* (Know the Warning Signs, National Alliance on Mental Illness)

- **Excessive fear or worry:** Everyone experiences fear and worry at times, but when these feelings become persistent, overwhelming, and interfere with daily life, it may be a sign of a deeper concern including anxiety, and phobias.
- **Extreme mood swings:** Significant emotional highs and lows that seem disproportionate to the situation at

hand can be a sign of a mood disorder like depression and bipolar disorder.

- **Persistent sadness or irritability:** While everyone has "off" days, persistent feelings of sadness or irritability could indicate a mental health concern like depression.
- **Feelings of worthlessness or guilt:** When worthlessness and guilt are disproportionate to the situation at hand, it can interfere with a person's ability to function normally. These feelings can be persistent and pervasive, affecting many aspects of a person's life, including self-perception, relationships, and work. They can also lead to a cycle of negative thinking that can worsen other mental health challenges.
- **Suicidal thoughts:** This is a serious warning sign indicating that a person is in significant emotional pain and may be at risk of ending their own life. Some of the most common illnesses associated with suicidal thoughts include major depression and post-traumatic stress disorder, a mental health concern caused by exposure to an incredibly stressful event like a natural disaster, accident, assault, terrorist event, war, and loss of a loved one.

It's important to note that not everyone with these challenges experiences suicidal thoughts. If you or someone you know is struggling with suicidal thoughts, it's important to seek help from a mental health professional. I can't stress enough how important it is to take thoughts or talk of suicide seriously; timely intervention could save a life.

WARNING SIGNS CONCERNING BEHAVIORAL WELL-BEING

By familiarizing ourselves with the following warning signs about one's behavior, we can learn how they *affect one's overall well-being*.

They are *not to be confused with a diagnosis or used as diagnostic criteria*. (Know the Warning Signs, National Alliance on Mental Illness)

- **Decreased energy or fatigue:** Mental health concerns like depression, anxiety, and sleep disorders such as insomnia or sleep apnea can cause changes in sleep patterns and energy levels. For example, someone dealing with insomnia may experience an ongoing lack of energy, leading to difficulty concentrating and making decisions. Depression can cause changes in the brain and body that make it harder for a person to sleep well, eat healthily, or engage in physical activity, contributing to feeling tired. Likewise, anxiety can cause constant worry or fear that can be mentally exhausting, leading to fatigue.
- **Dr. Jekyll and Mr. Hyde syndrome:** Named after the characters in Robert Louis Stevenson's novel "The Strange Case of Dr. Jekyll and Mr. Hyde," a sudden shift in behavior can indicate underlying issues including mood disorders, substance abuse, and manipulative tendencies. It can be deeply concerning when these sudden shifts happen because a lack of consistency and stability is disarming, confusing, and

frightening, to say the least. Any sudden or unexpected shift in someone's personality or behavior can create a sense of insecurity for others, potentially resulting in their feeling emotional and psychological distress.

- **Inability to handle daily problems or stress:** If a person consistently struggles to handle minor problems or stressors, it could indicate a lack of coping mechanisms, anxiety, feeling overwhelmed or pressured, or stress disorders. It's important to note that these symptoms can manifest differently for different people. Only a qualified healthcare professional can supply a correct diagnosis.

- **Passive aggression:** Passive aggression is the act of using subtle actions or comments to provoke or annoy someone while maintaining a guise of innocence. It is a defense mechanism used to protect oneself from confrontation or to assert control in a non-confrontational manner. Instead of openly addressing an issue, passive aggressive behavior *indirectly* expresses anger, frustration, or resentment, sometimes stemming from a fear of direct communication. It is often disguised as hurtful sarcasm, joking or kidding. Passive aggression can create a toxic dynamic, leading to a lack of effective communication, hurt feelings, and unresolved conflicts.

- **Substance use or abuse:** Using substances to cope with feelings or situations can signify a deeper issue. Substance abuse can be a sign of several mental health challenges including depression, anxiety, and "substance use disorder." It's important to note that substance abuse often co-occurs with other mental health challenges and can worsen them. (Dumain, T. 2022).

- **Significant changes in eating or sleeping habits:** Noticeable changes in appetite, weight, or sleep patterns can indicate several mental health concerns, including depression, anxiety, and eating disorders such as anorexia nervosa and bulimia. For instance, people with depression might experience insomnia, hypersomnia and significant weight loss or gain. Anxiety may cause sleep disturbances. The primary symptoms of an eating disorder are changes in eating habits and weight. It's important to note that various medical conditions can also cause these symptoms, so it's necessary to seek professional help for a proper diagnosis.

- **Unexplained physical ailments:** The mind and body are interconnected, so it is not surprising that mental health challenges can manifest as physical symptoms. For example, chronic pain can be a symptom of depression. It is important to note that physical symptoms can also be caused by other health conditions. *Everyone* experiences periods of fatigue in life, but consistently feeling low energy or weariness, especially when accompanied by mood, appetite, or sleep changes, might show a need to talk to a healthcare provider.

WARNING SIGNS CONCERNING COGNITIVE WELL-BEING

By understanding and recognizing the following warning signs concerning cognitive well-being, we can *gain greater insight into someone's state of well-being*.

These signs are *not to be confused with a diagnosis or used as diagnostic criteria*. (Know the Warning Signs, National Alliance on Mental Illness)

- **Confused thinking:** Anyone can experience confused thinking occasionally, but it could be a sign of a more significant issue if it's persistent or interferes with daily life. Confused thinking can indicate various mental health challenges, including delirium, often caused by substance abuse. Additionally, confusion in thinking can be a result of certain neurological conditions like dementia or a traumatic brain injury. It is important to consult with a healthcare professional for a proper evaluation and diagnosis.

- **Difficulty concentrating or making decisions:** Mental health conditions such as dementia, Alzheimer's disease, traumatic brain injury, attention deficit hyperactivity disorder, depression, and anxiety can affect cognitive functions like memory, attention, problem-solving, and decision-making. For example, someone with depression might struggle to concentrate because they're constantly feeling sad. A person struggling with anxiety might avoid making decisions due to excessive worry about potential outcomes.

- **Difficulty understanding reality:** Confused thinking, hallucinations, or delusions are common symptoms of something more serious, so it's essential to consult with a healthcare professional for an accurate diagnosis.
- **Inability to perceive changes in one's feelings, behavior, or personality:** Poor mental health can cause a disconnect between a person's perception of themselves and their behavior or emotional state. This lack of self-awareness can make it difficult for an individual to recognize that they are experiencing mental health challenges and may cause them to delay seeking help and treatment.

Compassionately Understanding Dementia: A Disorder That Demands Empathy

Based on my personal experiences with loved ones suffering from a form of confused thinking called dementia, I feel the need to address whether dementia is considered a mental illness.

Dementia is an umbrella term that refers to *neurological conditions* including Alzheimer's Disease, Vascular Dementia, Lewy Body Dementia, Parkinson's disease, and others. ***Dementia is considered a brain disorder.*** These conditions progressively impair the brain's ability to function, detrimentally affecting everyday life and activities and worsening over time. *(Alzheimer's Disease Fact Sheet, n.d.)*

Early detection and intervention play a crucial role in improving the quality of life for affected individuals. Timely medical intervention, planning, and access to resources and support can make a significant difference in their well-being. If you notice signs of confusion in someone, it's crucial to act. Please encourage them to seek medical advice. Remember, it's not about diagnosing them but guiding them towards professional help and offering emotional support during this potentially devastating time. Empathy and compassion are essential when providing care for individuals who struggle with dementia.

WARNING SIGNS CONCERNING RELATIONAL WELL-BEING

The following can *impact one's overall well-being*. By identifying the following warning signs we can *gain insight, clarity and make more informed decision about our relationships*.

They are *not to be confused with a diagnosis or used as diagnostic criteria*. (Know the Warning Signs, National Alliance on Mental Illness)

- **Difficulty keeping relationships:** Some psychological difficulties can lead to behaviors that strain relationships. For example, individuals with depression may become withdrawn and lose interest in activities they once enjoyed, making it difficult to engage with others and maintain healthy relationships. Similarly, individuals with anxiety may become irritable and easily agitated, creating tension in their interactions. Other relational well-being challenges may cause an over dependency on others for support and reassurance, which can be challenging for everyone involved. These behaviors are no one's fault, they are a sign that someone may benefit from professional help and need support to navigate challenges and improve their relationships.

- **Difficulty understanding or relating to others:** Struggling to relate or keep relationships can indicate several challenges, from difficulty hearing and seeing to social anxiety, and autism spectrum disorder. It's important to remember that indicators can vary significantly from person to person, and a professional diagnosis is necessary to identify any condition accurately.
- **Frequent conflicts:** Some mental health concerns may lead to increased irritability, mood swings, or difficulty managing emotions, all of which can contribute to arguments. Everyone has disagreements occasionally, but if conflicts become a regular occurrence, or become more heated, it could be a sign of a deeper issue.
- **Social withdrawal or isolation:** If a person consistently withdraws from social activities they once enjoyed, they may be experiencing peer pressure, bullying, or another type of emotional distress. It can also be indicative of underlying concerns including depression and anxiety. It is important to consult with a professional for a proper evaluation and diagnosis.

COGNITIVE DISTORTIONS: MISLEADING PERCEPTIONS OF REALITY

"Cognitive distortion" is a term used to describe the way our minds can sometimes play tricks on us, distorting our thoughts and perceptions of reality. It's like wearing a pair of glasses that make everything look lopsided. They are *patterns of thinking that may contribute to and worsen existing mental health challenges* and can have a significant impact on our emotions, behaviors, and relationships.

Imagine you're looking at a situation and your mind automatically jumps to the worst possible scenario, even though there's no evidence to support it. That's a cognitive distortion called "catastrophizing." It's like your mind is blowing things out of proportion and making you believe that everything is going to go wrong.

Another common cognitive distortion is "black-and-white thinking," where you see things as either all good or all bad, with no middle ground. This can lead to extreme judgments and rigid beliefs, making it difficult to see the nuances and complexities of a situation.

Cognitive distortions can lead to misunderstandings and miscommunications, resulting in feeling frustration and relationship dissatisfaction. For example, someone who consistently interprets innocent comments as personal attacks may become defensive and distant in their interactions with others, creating tension and strain in their relationships. Viewing gestures of kindness or support as insincere or manipulative can lead to a lack of trust and difficulty forming meaningful connections. Overall, the use of cognitive distortions can hinder effective communication, create barriers to understanding, and negatively impact any relationship

It's important to remember that cognitive distortions *are not a reflection of someone's character or intelligence.* They're simply patterns of thinking that can be influenced by various factors, such as past experiences, beliefs, and even mood. Recognizing and understanding these distortions can help us challenge and reframe our thoughts, allowing us to have a more balanced and realistic perspective. So, if you ever catch yourself falling into cognitive distortions, remember to be kind to yourself. It's not about blaming or criticizing anyone, but rather about acknowledging that our minds can sometimes distort our perception of reality, often automatically and unconsciously. By practicing self-compassion and seeking support we can learn to navigate our distortions and cultivate a healthier and more empathetic mindset.

Social psychologist Dr. Alice Boyes has created a list of fifty common cognitive distortions. Here are a few of them:

- **Applying double standards:** the tendency to hold oneself to different standards or expectations than others, judging oneself more harshly or leniently.

- **Jumping to conclusions:** assuming to know what others will say, do, or think, and that it will always be negative.

- **Engaging in a negativity bias:** noticing only the negative aspects of life and disregarding the positives.

- **Overgeneralizing:** applying the result of one isolated event to other areas of life.

- **Taking it personally:** seeing a personal attack in any unpleasant interaction (Boyes 2013).

Sure, any of these signs can be a normal part of life's ups and downs, however, if they persist or significantly impact one's daily life, it might be worth considering talking to a mental health professional. If you notice someone engaging in cognitive distortions regularly, here are a few steps you can take:

1. Educate yourself: Learn more about cognitive distortions and how they can change a person's thinking and behavior. This will help you better understand what the person may be going through.

2. Communicate openly: Approach the person in a non-judgmental and compassionate manner. Express your concern for their well-being and let them know that you've noticed certain patterns in their thinking.

3. Offer support: Let the person know that you're there for them and willing to listen. Encourage them to seek professional help, such as therapy or counseling, where they can learn strategies to challenge and overcome cognitive distortions.

4. Be patient: Changing thought patterns takes time and effort. Encourage the person to practice self-awareness and self-reflection and remind them that progress may not happen overnight.

Remember, it's important to respect the person's autonomy and boundaries. Ultimately, it's up to them to decide whether they want to seek help.

Chapter Four
IDENTIFYING POWER AND CONTROL RED FLAGS

Over the course of my life, I have come to realize that manipulative tactics can often be subtle and hard to recognize. It took me *years* to understand that insults, intimidation, isolation, monitoring, manipulating, gaslighting, exclusion, and physical or psychological abuse were just some of the warning signs of **coercive control**.

The concept of coercive control was first coined by Dr. Evan Stark in 1984. Coercive control as defined by Stark, is *a pattern of behavior that aims to strip away someone's freedom and sense of self*. It is not limited to violating someone's bodily integrity; it also infringes on their fundamental human rights.

"I once had a friend who was in a relationship with someone who constantly monitored her whereabouts, dictated what she could and could not wear, and isolated her from her friends and family. It was a subtle form of control that gradually worsened over time, and made her feel trapped and powerless." —Anonymous

In the past, coercive control was known as "domestic violence" and was perceived as being isolated "fights" or incidents of physical violence carried out by a current or former partner in one's home. Today, the concept of *coercive control* sheds light on deeper dynamics and highlights the systematic and ongoing nature of this type of abuse. Therapists define it as a form of domestic abuse that goes beyond physical violence and includes tactics that undermine one's autonomy, self-esteem, and freedom. Coercive control is used to dominate and control. It is characterized by a systematic pattern of behaviors that gradually erode the sense of self and independence and can have long-lasting negative effects on one's mental and emotional well-being.

As someone who has personally experienced coercive control in my relationships, I will describe it as the feeling of being held hostage and trapped in a distorted reality created by another person. It's like being caught in a maze of confusion, contradictions, and fear. Even when they are not physically present, surveillance will continue through constant phone calls, texts, and even using family members, including children, to report on you. This person seems all-powerful and omnipresent, so constant fear and confusion are at the core of your day. It's like living in a world where the rules constantly change (because they do,) stability is elusive, and you're always on edge. You don't know if you're "coming or going," and you live in a perpetual state of fight/flight/freeze/fawn, four common responses to stress or danger. Fight refers to the instinctual response of confronting the threat, while flight refers to the instinctual response of running away. Freeze refers to the instinctual response of becoming paralyzed in the face of danger, and fawn refers to the instinctual response of appeasing or pleasing the threat in order to escape harm.

As the cycle of control continues, one's emotional and physical health begin to feel the effects, and eventually symptoms of Complex Post Traumatic Stress Disorder (C-PTSD) may develop; a heightened sensitivity to specific emotional areas known as "triggers," which make navigating life more challenging. Those affected may experience shame, guilt, feelings of responsibility for the trauma, difficulty controlling their emotions, and a loss of focus. We'll talk at length about C-PTSD in chapter eleven.

Victims of coercive control live under constant scrutiny, subjected to never-ending criticism, and their every action is examined against an unpredictable and ever-changing standard. Rules are based on narrow and stereotypical expectations of how to act in various situations, such as cooking, housekeeping, parenting, sexual performance, and socializing. Yet, it extends beyond the home, because with the help of technology, surveillance can happen anywhere you go. Metaphorically speaking you may become "brainwashed," internalizing the ever-changing rules as best you can and adapting your behavior accordingly. "Controlled" becomes the constant framework in which you live your life, so you focus on *them*, pleasing and appeasing to feel a sense of safety and stability, and losing your *self* in the process. The strength and courage required to live like this, and continue to function daily, is staggering.

Coercive control is used for personal gain, gratification, and the sheer enjoyment of controlling you and undermining your autonomy and freedom. It can manifest in several ways, and the tactics are almost endless. Many of these tactics were previously mentioned in chapter two, as warning signs of toxicity. We'll explore them deeper in this chapter.

UNDERSTANDING THE TACTICS OF COERCIVE CONTROL

Now, let's explore a list of tactics that are commonly associated with coercive control:

Abuses privilege: Acts superior and subjugates or exploits your race, gender, gender identity, sexual orientation, socio-economic status, disability, or immigration status. They feel entitled to everything being on their terms and treat you like a servant.

Criticizes your appearance: Criticizing your appearance can be an indicator of coercive control and emotional abuse because it is a way to undermine your self-esteem and cause you to feel inadequate. They are trying to control how you perceive yourself and manipulate your self-worth.

Emotionally abuses: Raging, name-calling, degradation, projection, shaming, humiliation, guilt-tripping, invalidating your feelings, needs, and boundaries, using cruel insults disguised as humor, and blaming you for relationship problems are all forms of emotional abuse.

Intimidates: Reinforces your fear by using bullying tones, statements, postures, gestures, or a "look." Examples of intimidation include blocking your way if you try to exit, aggressive driving, and ignoring your boundaries and your non-consent.

Isolates: Isolates you from friends, family, personal goals, and interests by criticizing, devaluing, making fun of, or distrusting the people you hold dear. Dictates where you go, what you do, when and with whom you speak.

Financially exploits: Watches your spending, makes all significant financial decisions, shared assets are in *their name only*, you're prevented from earning or keeping personal income, building credit, and accessing bank accounts, and your professional aspirations are unsupported or blocked.

Gaslights: A manipulative tactic and form of emotional abuse that uses mind games in an attempt to control your beliefs, feelings, thoughts, perceptions, actions, and reactions. A gaslighter typically maintains a calm, rational demeanor when they gaslight, leaving you feeling insecure and irrational by comparison. The focus of concern is shifted off their abusive behavior and onto your supposed emotional and psychological instability.

They insist that you lie about your relationship: You may feel pressured to hide your true feelings and compromise your values for the sake of the relationship, or its image. They don't want to draw attention from anyone who might interfere, which suggests that they are more concerned with maintaining appearances than building a healthy and authentic connection with you. Lying to others about the nature of your relationship can lead to a toxic and manipulative dynamic.

Lacks empathy: As mentioned in chapters two and five, empathy describes the ability to recognize or identify with the feelings and needs of others. It's the ability to understand another person's thoughts and feelings from their point of view. Empathetic people *actively share* in a person's emotional experience.

If you notice that someone is consistently showing a lack of empathy, it's a red flag. Those without empathy may not be capable of understanding your emotions or supplying emotional support when you need it.

Lies and Triangulates: Under the guise of concern, they lie to try to discredit you, and suggest that you are unstable. They flirt with others or cheat, then gaslight you to confuse and control you.

Triangulation, previously mentioned in chapter two and described as a key indicator of toxicity, involves playing one person against another by controlling the amount and type of communication they have with each other. It's often used to control individuals in a relationship. Of the three, only one of them controls the narrative between the other two. It can be emotionally damaging, leading to feelings of insecurity, mistrust, and isolation, and generating rivalry, confusion, tension, and even competition between the two individuals being manipulated.

Love bombs: As previously mentioned in chapter two, love-bombing is a manipulative tactic to gain control and power. It involves showering you with excessive affection, attention, and compliments to create an intense and overwhelming emotional bond. Love-bombing can be incredibly deceptive and emotionally damaging because the love-bomber is not genuinely interested in your well-being or happiness. They use these tactics to control you.

Monitors and uses surveillance: Checking your location or devices goes against the principles of privacy, trust, respect, and personal boundaries. When a person needs to constantly watch or surveil the other, an atmosphere of suspicion and distrust is created. This behavior can stem from distrust, jealousy, or insecurity. It is important to remember that a healthy relationship is built on mutual trust and respect, where both individuals feel secure and valued. Monitoring or surveilling erode trust and create an imbalance of power, where one feels controlled or lives with a constant violation of their privacy.

Possessive: A lack of trust and respect in a relationship can lead to possessiveness, a controlling behavior showing a sense of ownership over you, which can be detrimental to your well-being.

Questions your friends and family: A lack of trust and respect in your personal boundaries can make you feel like your privacy is being invaded and that your relationships are being analyzed. When someone questions your friends or family about you, it may be a sign of possessiveness and control, and may cause feelings of insecurity and unease for you.

Uses fear or physical harm: These tactics are manipulative and abusive, used to control or intimidate.

Uses psychological cruelty: Gaslighting, manipulation, emotional abuse, verbal abuse, isolation, and constant criticism are examples of emotional brutality. It is important to note that every relationship is unique, and the presence of these behaviors does not necessarily mean that the relationship is abusive. However, if you or someone you know is experiencing any of these forms of psychological cruelty, it is important to seek support and consider professional help.

Uses threats: These include explicit or veiled threats to instill a sense of fear concerning your finances, housing, personal security, immigration status, reputation, or physical safety.

COERCIVE CONTROL: EFFECTS ON PHYSICAL AND MENTAL WELL-BEING

Coercive control can be far more sinister than other types of abuse because it's hard to detect and does not look like the "typical" forms of mistreatment associated with abuse; there are no outward signs of bruising, broken bones, cuts etc.

More examples of coercive control

- Does not allow you to work or attend school
- Restricts your access to transportation (I once had a partner who removed my car's distributor cap, preventing the engine from starting whenever I had plans to meet up with friends.)
- Takes your phone
- Uses intimacy and sex as methods to control you
- Monitors your health and body (possibly monitors your monthly cycle to know when you're most likely to become pregnant)
- Changes passwords to lock you out of accounts
- Holds your personal possessions for ransom as punishment or as a means of emotional blackmail.
- Withholding, damaging, or keeping your belongings from you

It's interesting to note that the controlling person may *reward you* with compliments, praise, or even love bombing when you comply with their controlling tactics!

If you are or have been afraid that someone may become violent with you, or their controlling behavior has adversely affected your daily activities or the way you live, you may be experiencing coercive control. For instance, if you have noticed a decline in your physical or mental well-being, have changed your socializing habits, or how you handle household tasks and errands, or made modifications in your daily commute to school or work, or adjustments in how you care for your children, all as a means to ensure your safety, it is possible that you are dealing with coercive control.

Ongoing coercion can have severe and long-lasting effects on your physical and mental well-being. It can lead to power imbalances in your relationship by violating your fundamental human rights.

BREAKING FREE: OVERCOMING COERCIVE CONTROL TO RECLAIM YOUR LIFE

Recognizing these signs early is important to protect yourself from entering an unhealthy or dangerous relationship. It can be incredibly difficult to leave this type of situation, especially if your self-esteem and self-worth have been deeply negatively affected, or if your access to money or transportation has been restricted.

If you find yourself in this kind of situation, it's important to reach out for help. **In the US**, call the National Domestic Violence Hotline: Hours- 24/7. Language-: English, Spanish, and 200+ through interpretation service 800-799-7233. **Here is a list of help in Europe** in 46 countries: https://wave-network.org/list-of-helplines-in-46-countries. **In England, Scotland, Wales, and Northern Ireland**: https://www.womensaid.org.uk/womens-aid-directory.

Speaking with a relational trauma professional may provide you with the support and guidance to navigate this challenging situation. (Tanasugarn, A., 2022) Remember, every relationship is unique. Trust your instincts and seek support if you notice any concerning patterns or controlling behaviors.

Chapter Five
THE IMPORTANCE OF EMOTIONAL EMPATHY

The lack of empathy is a huge red flag.

Empathy plays a crucial role in any healthy relationship, and its absence can result in your feeling isolated, emotionally neglected, and dissatisfied in the relationship.

Indicators of a lack of empathy include disregarding or downplaying your emotions, being unable to identify with your perspective, consistently prioritizing their wants and needs above yours, and displaying a lack of interest or concern for your well-being. It is essential to trust your instincts and recognize these behaviors early to avoid involvement in a relationship that may be emotionally exhausting and detrimental to your well-being.

EMPATHY'S ROLE IN RELATIONSHIP DYNAMICS

Empathy is "the ability to understand another person's thoughts and feelings from their point of view, rather than your own" (acuityinsights 2020). When we're empathetic, we actively share a person's emotional experience. It's different from sympathy, which is feeling concerned about someone's well-being *while maintaining a healthy and appropriate amount of emotional distance.*

Individuals may struggle with a lack of empathy due to influences like exposure to trauma, upbringing, and life experiences. While some individuals may naturally have a higher capacity for empathy, others may have a lower capacity and a healthy mental status. It is important to note that empathy is a spectrum, and most of us can develop and enhance our empathetic abilities through awareness and practice.

Empathetic deficiencies are often revealed during times of crisis, conflict, or high stress. When feeling pressured, emotions become more challenging to control, and the absence of empathy can become evident as a noticeable lack of care about others.

TYPES OF EMPATHY IN RELATIONSHIPS

In the realm of social psychology, it is understood that there are *two types* of empathy: emotional and cognitive.

Emotional empathy is characterized by our ability to personally feel the same emotion as another individual. It entails immersing ourselves in their perspective and genuinely experiencing what they are feeling. For example, if you see someone crying and it elicits a genuine sense of sadness within you, you are feeling emotional empathy.

Some individuals have the ability to perceive and react to another person's situation, without experiencing emotions themselves, and it's critical to understand the difference (Baskin-Sommers, Krusemark, and Ronningstam 2014).

For someone to feel **emotional empathy**, they must be able to:

- feel the same emotion as another person. For example, seeing someone in the act of embarrassing themselves and feeling embarrassed for them.
- feel distressed in response to the person's feelings
- feel compassion for the person

Cognitive empathy refers to this ability to intellectually understand that someone may be experiencing a specific emotion, without personally experiencing any emotional response to this understanding. It requires a basic understanding of emotions (Hodges and Myers, 2007).

When someone uses a simple visual perspective to guess what you're feeling, they're using cognitive empathy. For example, if they look at you and notice your eyes are swollen and red, probably from crying, they may correctly guess that you are feeling sad. If someone using cognitive empathy knows a person well enough, they can make educated guesses about how that person feels and potentially use that knowledge to hurt them as well. Daniel Goleman (author of the book "Emotional Intelligence") writes that torturers require cognitive empathy to figure out how to hurt a person best. Similarly, when a person who lacks empathy acts kindly, they may be rooting out your hopes, wishes, and dreams and use the information to intentionally hurt you later.

EXPLORING EMPATHETIC BEHAVIORS AND TRAITS

When we feel pain resulting from someone else's emotions, it can be highly distressing. There is a delicate balance to be looked for and kept when it comes to feeling empathy for others, and it is important to not allow our empathy for others to negatively affect our own well-being.

"One day, our neighborhood experienced a pretty bad flood and many homes were ruined. The community came together to support and help those in need, but one neighbor showed no concern or willingness to lend a hand. He continued with his daily routine, unaffected by those suffering around him. It was clear that he lacked the ability to care or empathize. His indifference isolated him from the rest of the community, and it left a lasting impression on me." —Anonymous

A fascinating discovery from the largest genetic study on empathy conducted to date is the identification of the "empathy gene." This groundbreaking research, published in Translational Psychiatry on March 12, 2018, by Warrier et al., revealed that our level of empathy is influenced to some extent by genetics.

PART II:
UNMASKING ABUSE

Content Warning:

This section contains frank discussions of relationship red flags, mental health challenges, and other sensitive topics including neglect and abuse. Please be aware that reading about these issues may be difficult for some readers.

Reader discretion is advised.

Chapter Six
THE FOUR ELEMENTS OF ABUSE

By understanding the definition of abuse and recognizing what abuse looks like, we can protect ourselves and others from harmful situations and relationships. Abuse can take many forms, including physical, emotional, verbal, and even financial. It can be subtle and manipulative, making it difficult to identify at times. But by being aware of the signs and symptoms, we can empower ourselves to take action and seek help when needed. By recognizing and understanding abuse, we can work together to create a safer and more compassionate world for everyone.

IDENTIFYING ABUSE AND PROTECTING OURSELVES AND OTHERS

As a domestic violence counselor, I had the privilege of working with many courageous women navigating abusive relationships. One of the critical concepts we focused on was "the cycle of abuse," which served as a framework to understand the patterns of behavior leading up to and including an abusive event. By empowering women to recognize the patterns and name which stage they were currently in, we aimed to equip them with the tools to create a preemptive strategy to avoid or cope with an upcoming abusive incident.

Recognizing abuse is not only about protecting ourselves, but also about showing empathy and support to those who may be experiencing it.

"I was in a relationship with someone who had a history of abusive behavior. The tension between us would often build up over small disagreements, and he would become increasingly irritable and critical. One day, during an argument, his anger escalated to physical violence.

After the abusive incident, he was sorry, apologized profusely, and promised that it would never happen again. He showered me with affection and gifts and tried to make up for his actions. I was desperate for things to change, so I believed him, and hoped our relationship could improve. In the honeymoon phase, he was like a different person; attentive, loving, and trying to control his anger. But as time went on, the tension started building again, and the cycle repeated itself." —Anonymous

THE CYCLE OF ABUSE: IMPACT AND IMPLICATIONS

Dr. Lenore Walker first proposed the cycle of abuse in 1979 after conducting extensive interviews with 1,500 domestic violence survivors. Through her research, she discovered that the women all shared similar abusive scenarios and a recognizable pattern of how the abusive events unfolded. Drawing from this, she developed the concept of a cycle which has since become a valuable resource in understanding and addressing the dynamics of abuse.

Four elements were present for each of the abuse survivors:

1. Tension building

2. Abusive incident

3. Remorse

4. Honeymoon

The Honeymoon Period continues directly into Tension Building, and the cycle repeats itself uninterrupted. Every cycle shares the same four phases, but each cycle's details differ from the earlier ones. From one abuse cycle to the next, each of the four stages and the cycle itself can last different amounts of time or include behaviors that are unique to those of the last time.

The following diagram is based on Walker's Cycle of Abuse.

1. Tension Building   2. Abusive Incident

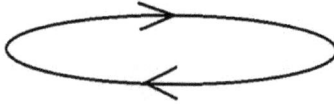

4. Honeymoon   3. Remorse

(Walker, L.E.,1979)

The first phase is the "Tension Building" period. During this phase, the target senses growing strain in the relationship and becomes anxious, highly alert, and guarded. There is an unshakeable feeling that there will be an abusive incident soon. Hence, the target tries to control the environment to keep the abuser happy and calm. I remember a time when I would have attempted to control the *weather* had I thought it would keep my partner calm and stable.

In phase two, the abusive incident occurs, which may be physical, mental, spiritual, emotional, verbal, or financial. Examples include physical violence (things like pushing, hitting, choking, punching, kicking) and mental, spiritual, emotional, and verbal abuse, including name-calling, gaslighting, threats, intimidation, angry outbursts, arguing, blaming, and withholding love, affection, and attention.

The third phase is the "Remorse" period. The abuser apologizes, makes excuses, and promises that the abuse will never happen again. The target is showered with love, affection, and attention and sometimes gifts and other tokens of affection are given as indicators of sorrow or regret. This is a form of love bombing.

The "Honeymoon" is a period of calm while the abuser tries to make the target feel loved, safe, and secure again. The Honeymoon will continue for an undetermined amount of time, the length of which may change in each cycle.

This entire cycle will continuously be repeated, often over years, until it is intentionally interrupted by one of the two participants. One way of interrupting the cycle is to leave the relationship.

THE NARCISSISTIC CYCLE OF ABUSE: A DIFFERENT DYNAMIC

Narcissists hold a distorted self-image and have high conflict personalities. They do things that most of us would not, such as thoughtlessly spend other people's money, humiliate a child, sabotage a coworker, or verbally attack a stranger (Eddy 2018). They consider themselves superior and are comfortable putting down, insulting, and demeaning others to feel powerful and boost their self-image. They tend to be selfish and do not reciprocate kind gestures. They're demanding, needing almost constant admiration and attention from anyone in their vicinity (a.k.a. narcissistic supply).

Additionally, they waste time trying to impress anyone who will listen. They break promises, make excuses, and take credit for others' ideas or work. They enjoy bullying and are willing to speak disapprovingly of someone behind their back but only have positive things to say in their presence. These traits can make narcissists exhausting for those of us who live and work with them.

Unlike the traditional cycle of abuse, the narcissistic abuse cycle *lacks the Remorse phase.* This absence can be attributed to the narcissist's unwillingness to accept responsibility for their actions, instead opting to shift the blame onto their target.

Remembering that narcissists have an insatiable need to feel superior and "right" in every situation, coupled with their inherent lack of empathy, prevents them from experiencing feelings of remorse. Remorsefulness requires empathy, sympathy, and the willingness to take responsibility for our actions (Hammond 2018).

The is no period of remorse in the narcissistic cycle of abuse, and it diverges significantly from Walker's cycle in phase four.

The following diagram is based on Christine Hammond's Narcissistic Cycle of Abuse.

1. Narcissistic Injury	2. Abusive Incident
4. Narcissist Empowered	3. Role Reversal

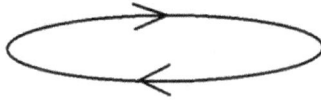

(Hammond, C. 2018)

In phase one, a narcissistic injury occurs; the abuser feels rejected, threatened, jealous, abandoned, disrespected, or any feeling that challenges their superiority. The target feels anxious and tries to appease and please, much like in phase one of Walker's Cycle of Abuse.

As in Walker's Cycle, phase two is also an abusive incident, which may be physical, mental, spiritual, emotional, verbal, or financial. Examples include physical violence (things like pushing, hitting, choking, punching, kicking) and mental, spiritual, emotional, and verbal abuse, including name-calling, gaslighting, threats, intimidation, angry outbursts, arguing, blaming, and withholding love, affection, and attention.

Phase three takes on a completely different dynamic. When a narcissist is involved, the roles in the remorse stage are *reversed; the narcissist assumes the role of the victim,* while the *target* is expected to apologize and appease. As

THE FOUR ELEMENTS OF ABUSE

the cycle progresses into the fourth phase, the narcissistic behaviors become more pronounced, and the abuse cycle continues unless someone intentionally breaks it.

To break free from this cycle, the target must change their behavior by refusing to accept the role reversal. In other words, they must no longer shoulder the blame or accept the role of abuser.

There are other subtle ways that narcissists try to control or manipulate:

- belittling, criticizing, and name-calling

- patronizing and condescending

- publicly or privately embarrassing you

- threatening you or others

- ordering you to do things, taking away your choices

- controlling money or your access to it

- monitoring and controlling your whereabouts

- exhibiting scary, emotional outbursts

- acting on jealousy

- using manipulative or guilt-inducing ploys

- isolating you from friends, family members, or social connections

- displaying indifference to your mental or physical needs

- denying or trivializing your feelings

Any combination of these may lower or annihilate your self-esteem and cause you to feel fearful and ashamed (McBride 2018).

Chapter Seven
INVISIBLE AND ANXIOUS: THE SILENT TREATMENT

The silent treatment inflicts deep emotional pain.

It is a form of emotional abuse where you are intentionally ignored as a means of punishment and control. It can be used by anyone who wants to exert power or manipulate a situation. (Eisenberger et al., 2004).

A SILENT PUNISHMENT

The silent treatment, also known as stonewalling, giving the cold shoulder, emotional withholding and shunning, is tactic employing a hurt and rescue approach. It's often used to teach a lesson or to manipulate behavior over a period of time (Eisenberger et al., 2004). For those who have experienced this type of abuse, it may trigger a fear of abandonment and create ongoing anxiety (Saeed, K., 2019).

When I was seventeen years old, I went through a painfully challenging experience with my mother, who subjected me to her version of the silent treatment for three months. It was not the first time, but it was the longest. Throughout that period, she completely ignored me. It was as if I did not exist and it was humiliating, confusing and heartbreaking.

Desperate for interaction, I occasionally tried to break the silence and was met with cold rejection each time. Whenever I tried to engage, she avoided eye contact and would not acknowledge my existence. It was clear that this was a punishment, although I was unsure of the reason. My efforts to reconcile remained unsuccessful.

"Remove the veils so I might see what is happening here and not be intoxicated by my stories and my fears."
—Elizabeth Lesser

Eventually, the silent treatment ended just as mysteriously as it had begun. She broke the silence with a trivial comment, signaling the end of the banishment. I never understood what I had done to deserve such extreme measures, and I spent a lot of time obsessing over it, replaying old conversations and scenarios. Of course, we never talked about it, and her reasons are still a mystery to this day. I've wondered if it was simply a display of power, meant to demoralize and unsettle me.

UNRESOLVED SILENCE: THE LASTING IMPACT

Experiencing the silent treatment can have a profound impact on your mental and emotional well-being, as research has shown with brain scans. For those of us who have already experienced abandonment by someone significant, the silent treatment is another form of abandonment. It can feel unbearable and burning questions like "Do I matter?" and "Does anyone love me?" consume us.

Living with a fear of abandonment can result in a range of debilitating symptoms like anxiety, insomnia, difficulty concentrating, and an overall sense of unease. It becomes incredibly challenging to function in academic or professional settings when someone significant to you actively ignores you. The silent treatment can push us into survival mode, triggering panic attacks, changes in appetite, heart palpitations, nightmares, depression, confusion, and obsessive thoughts. Consequently, our focus shifts to the needs of the person ignoring us, and we become motivated to appease them to restore a sense of stability and safety, and alleviate our pain.

"I once had a colleague who would often resort to giving me the silent treatment whenever we had a disagreement. Instead of addressing the issue and finding a resolution, they would completely shut down and refuse to communicate. This silent treatment made it incredibly difficult to resolve conflicts and maintain a healthy working relationship." —Anonymous

The silent treatment is a powerful tool used to assert dominance. Being ignored can make us doubt our value and worth, as we feel increasingly anxious. Our self-esteem and confidence gradually erode, leading us to believe that we are undeserving of better treatment. We settle for scraps of affection, which can perpetuate trauma bonds, the powerful emotional connections that are created between two individuals undergoing cycles of abuse together. We may become trapped in a progression of emotional manipulation and mistreatment.

If you find yourself in a situation where you are subjected to the silent treatment, there are several things you can do. First, recognize and acknowledge the behavior for what it is - a form of emotional abuse and manipulation. It can be helpful to seek support from trusted friends, family members, and therapists or counselors who can supply guidance, validation, and help. It's also important to start setting boundaries and communicate assertively with the person giving the silent treatment, expressing how their behavior is affecting you and what you need from them. It is crucial to prioritize your well-being and safety, and it may be necessary to consider removing yourself from the relationship altogether.

The silent treatment can have a profound impact on our emotional well-being. However, it is only one aspect of a complex web of emotional manipulation. In the next chapter, we will examine another devious tactic known as gaslighting. By exploring the intricacies of gaslighting, we can gain a deeper understanding of emotional abuse and the lasting effects it can have.

Chapter Eight
GASLIGHTING: PLANTING THE SEEDS OF SELF DOUBT

This chapter aims to unravel the complexities of gaslighting, a form of psychological exploitation that leaves its victims questioning their own reality. As we explore gaslighting's subtle yet devastating effects, we'll get a glimpse the power it can hold over our self-perception.

Gaslighting is a manipulative tactic and form of emotional abuse that uses mind games in an attempt to control your beliefs, feelings, thoughts, perceptions, actions, and reactions. A gaslighter typically keeps a calm, rational demeanor and leaves you feeling insecure and irrational by comparison. Manipulating your observations and emotions gives a gaslighter significant amounts of power and control. Because it reduces our ability to think critically and make sound decisions, gaslighting leaves us unsure of our reality. It is the most treacherous form of manipulation because it undermines our very core, our sense of self.

The term was borrowed from the 1938 stage play "Gaslight," in which a husband tries to drive his wife insane by dimming their home's gas-powered lights and denying it when she notices. She begins to doubt her perception, judgment, memory, and reality, leading her to believe she is losing her grip on sanity.

Narcissists and people with narcissistic traits employ gaslighting in an effort to get an emotional response that feeds and supports their ego and sense of superiority. As mentioned in chapter six, it is known as narcissistic supply, and is crucial for a narcissist's self-esteem. Any emotional reaction including pain, sadness, fear, joy, happiness, and anger can serve as a form of narcissistic supply.

Not all individuals who engage in gaslighting behavior are narcissists. Anyone can use gaslighting tactics. Additionally, gaslighting can occur unintentionally or stem from a desire "to be right" rather than a desire to control another person (Drescher, 2023).

When you're gaslighted, you may not fully understand what is happening, but you have a sense of confusion, feeling that something is not right. It can feel incredibly stressful and frustrating, causing you to doubt yourself, question your memory, and feel on edge. It's a profoundly unsettling experience.

Some signs that show you've experienced gaslighting are:

- constantly questioning your memory or perception of events

- feeling confused or unsure about what is real

- doubting your judgment and decision-making abilities

- feeling like you are "losing your mind"

- experiencing a sense of powerlessness or helplessness

- feeling isolated or cut off from friends and family

- having your feelings and experiences invalidated or dismissed

- feeling like you are constantly "walking on eggshells" and afraid to speak up about it

- noticing a pattern of lies or inconsistencies in the gaslighter's behavior

- feeling emotionally drained or exhausted from trying to make sense of your gaslighting experience

Ongoing gaslighting can have adverse emotional effects on us. Struggling to resolve what *you know* to be real with *what you are told* is real creates uncertainty, and you may start doubting your memory, and past and current experiences. You may feel confused and doubt your senses and judgment. This *internal conflict between these two versions of reality* (theirs and yours) can cause you to experience **cognitive dissonance**, a type of mental stress that results from grappling with discrepancies between what you believe to be true and **what you are told** to believe is true. It's that surreal moment when you **know** that you heard or saw X, but you're told that you saw Y. You know what you saw but you still question it; because you now doubt your senses and your ability to remember accurately.

"I was in a relationship where my significant other would constantly manipulate my perception of reality. She would deny things she said or did, making me question my own memory and sanity. She would twist situations and tell me I was overreacting or being too sensitive. It was a constant cycle of confusion and self-doubt and it took me a long time to realize that I was being gaslighted." —Anonymous

HOW GASLIGHTING UNDERMINES PERSONAL GROWTH AND SELF-TRUST

Persistent gaslighting may result in our feeling depressed, anxious, helpless, hopeless, and exhausted. In severe cases, we may experience a blurred sense of self and a dreamlike state of reality. Thinking becomes more challenging, and decision-making and problem-solving abilities are impaired. Despite these struggles, the gaslighter will continue playing mind games, manipulating our memories and experiences. Over time, we may lose touch with our sense of self and experience dissociation; the disconnection from sensory input, events, and sense of self, resulting in feeling disconnected from your identity and surroundings. Eventually, ***your perception of reality may ultimately*** *depend on the gaslighter's interpretations*, leading to a further loss of self.

PRESERVING THE SENSE OF SELF: OVERCOMING THE EFFECTS

Persistent gaslighting can lead to a loss of self-confidence and self-esteem, as we continue to doubt our observations, and constantly second-guess ourselves, distrusting our five senses and our memory. Additionally, gaslighting can erode our relationships, or create power imbalances, as the gaslighter gains more control over our thoughts and actions. Overall, the effects of continued gaslighting can be deeply damaging to one's mental and emotional well-being, and as we become more unsure of what is correct and true, we may develop the need to control other aspects of our lives.

If we challenge their behavior, we may risk potential retaliation and loss of the relationship. In an attempt to avoid these consequences, we may rationalize or justify their behavior to maintain a sense of stability and security, even if it contradicts our own beliefs and values. This is an example of self-gaslighting.

SELF-GASLIGHTING: CARRYING ON THE TRADITION

Self-gaslighting is a profoundly personal experience that involves deceiving ourselves.

It's the act of minimizing or dismissing someone's hurtful behavior, possibly making excuses for their actions, convincing yourself that an event did not happen or that it happened differently than you remember it, or accepting a revised version of past events that contradicts your memories. We engage in self-gaslighting by believing someone's negative behavior or choices were our fault. We may convince ourselves that we provoked their hurtful actions, accept responsibility, and make excuses for their hurtful behavior, absolving them of accountability.

Refusing to accept gaslighting in any form, whether from yourself, or someone else, is a decisive step towards reclaiming your truth and overall well-being.

PART III:
EMOTIONAL WELL-BEING: ASSESSING AND MAINTAINING YOUR SAFETY

Content Warning:

This section contains frank discussions of relationship red flags, mental health challenges, and other sensitive topics including neglect and abuse. Please be aware that reading about these issues may be difficult for some readers.

Reader discretion is advised.

Chapter Nine
EVALUATING POTENTIAL DANGER

When it comes to protecting yourself from mistreatment, recognizing the signs is paramount to prioritize your safety. (Duignan, n.d.) Trusting your instincts and listening to your body's signals is key. If something feels off or uncomfortable, it's necessary to acknowledge and explore those feelings, even if they're scary. Our bodies can hold valuable information that our minds may overlook. If you notice any warning signs, acknowledge them no matter how badly you may want to dismiss them. Whether it's now or in the future, eventually you will have to make decisions about what you've discovered.

When evaluating whether someone will be a positive influence in your life, there are some key aspects to consider. According to Bill Eddy, the social worker who developed the WEB Method, there are three specific areas of concern.

PAY ATTENTION TO THEIR <u>W</u>ORDS

Pay attention to the language and vocabulary that they use. Individuals with toxic traits often engage in excessive criticism, blame-shifting, and manipulation. They may also use derogatory or demeaning language towards others. Look for highly positive or negative language when they describe you or others, which could suggest all-or-nothing, black-and-white thinking. Additionally, watch for words that may show a lack of emotional empathy or interest in others, and words that portray them as victims; deceived, targeted, and wounded. Notice if they virtue signal, the not-so-humble bragging about their morals and values, named in chapter two as an indicator of toxicity.

PAY ATTENTION TO YOUR EMOTIONS

How do you feel when you are around this individual? Do you feel confused? Drained? Hurt? Defeated? Misunderstood? Stupid? Inadequate? Bullied? Mocked? Belittled? Humiliated? These emotions serve as powerful warning signs, signaling potential risk to your well-being.

Do you find yourself feeling overwhelmed or unable to think clearly when you're around them? If they consistently monopolize conversations, dismiss alternate viewpoints, and redirect the discussion towards themselves, it may feel more like you're having a debate, and there's exhausting effort needed to shift the topic or disengage. You may feel unheard, misunderstood, disregarded, or even ridiculed if you dare to challenge or disagree with them.

Do they excessively shower you with affection and compliments? Are they incredibly charming? As mentioned earlier, love-bombing is insincere, and individuals who excessively flatter or praise may have manipulative intentions. Charm can be a warning sign of a dishonest or controlling individual, and it's important to be cautious of excessive charm, as it can indicate a hidden agenda or a desire for control. It is important to take your time and carefully look at this individual in various situations. Over time, you will gain a better understanding of their true nature and intentions, and you will know whether they are trustworthy.

PAY ATTENTION TO THEIR BEHAVIOR

Look for patterns of behavior that indicate a lack of empathy or disregard for others' feelings and well-being. This includes the tendency to control, mistreat or exploit others, or a consistent lack of accountability for their actions. It is important to see how they treat others and how they handle conflicts or disagreements. Individuals with toxic traits tend to escalate situations, becoming aggressive or hostile when faced with challenges or differing opinions.

"I was at a social gathering where a friend of mine started talking about how much they care about the environment and how they always recycle and use eco-friendly products. But throughout the conversation, it was clear that they were only saying these things to impress others. It felt insincere and like they were just trying to indicate their supposed moral superiority rather than genuinely caring about the environment." —Anonymous

Notice if they blame others for their mistakes or poor choices, or if they encourage others to admire them. Are they prone to a cycle of intentionally hurting your feelings and then making up for it with acts of kindness?

Don't fall in love with someone's potential. You're looking for an equal, not a project.

When it comes to staying safe in relationships, it's not only important to pay attention to their words, your emotions, and their behavior. Dr. Ramini Durvasula, psychologist, professor, media expert, and author suggests asking the following two questions, and *notice how you feel in your body* when they respond.

The first question is, "Tell me the story of you." This question allows the person to share their life experiences, values, and beliefs *as a narrative* rather than answering yes/no questions. This open-ended format encourages more authentic and revealing answers.

The second question is, "How do you spend your days?" This one allows them to talk about their daily routines, hobbies, and interests, supplying a *glimpse into their lifestyle, values, and priorities,* aiding you in understanding who they are. As with the first question, it avoids judgmental undertones.

As they answer, *pay attention to how you feel in your body*. Trust your gut instincts and listen to the information your body is giving you. If something feels "off" or uncomfortable, it's essential to acknowledge and explore those feelings. I'll say it again: our bodies often hold valuable information that our minds can overlook.

In addition to listening to your body, be *mindful of any red flags* you notice in their responses. Signs of *contempt, a lack of empathy, simmering or outright anger, or feelings of victimization* can indicate potential issues.

When interpreting their answers, *be aware of any tendency to make the pieces fit together* or minimize or ignore warning signs. It's essential to be honest with yourself and not create narratives that don't align with the reality. Just be aware of the stories you tell yourself about *their* story, is all I'm saying.

If you have a five-hour conversation after the first date and feel amazing because they are SO into you, take another look at that. It may seem like a positive sign of interest but consider the possible underlying intentions. Narcissists and other people with toxic traits are extremely skilled at gathering information to manipulate and play with other's emotions. If they ask *intrusive questions* or *disregard your discomfort or boundaries*, make note of that; it could indicate a disrespectful attitude and indifference for your feelings and well-being.

Lastly, pay attention to how they respond *when you enforce your boundaries*. If they become hostile, argumentative, threatening, victimized, lose interest, or dismissive, you may be talking to a person with toxic traits.

Always trust your instincts and prioritize your well-being in your relationships.

FROM AWARENESS TO ACTION: SAFEGUARDING YOUR WELL-BEING

During my time as a domestic violence counselor, in my role as court advocate, I often had the opportunity to support individuals who were in the process of leaving abusive relationships. One piece of advice we counselors often shared with these brave individuals was ***to approach their new relationships with caution and keep things casual for at least the first six months*** to see how the new person of interest handles themselves in various situations. Watching how a person expresses a range of emotions over several months is highly beneficial to you for several reasons. By witnessing their emotions, especially *anger, frustration, sadness, and fear* firsthand:

You can gain valuable insight into how they express and manage their feelings, giving you a better understanding of their emotional maturity level, communication skills, and interaction style.

1. You can gauge their ability to handle conflicts and assess your compatibility in that area.

How do they handle difficult or stressful situations? Do they remain calm? Are they willing to negotiate and compromise? Are they respectful of your and others' perspectives and feelings? Do they honor your boundaries? Do they accept responsibility when they make a mistake? Do they apologize? Observations like these can supply valuable insights into someone's emotional intelligence and how they might handle future struggles.

Understand that only a select few deserve your time, energy, and attention.

Dedicate sufficient time to see a wide range of emotions, while evaluating how they are managed. By taking the time to watch and reflect, you can better understand how they express and manage their emotions, how they handle demanding situations, and whether they show empathy and understanding towards others. If any warning signs become clear, you have an opportunity to step back.

Here are some steps you can begin to take right now to safeguard your well-being:

Establish boundaries: Take the time to define your boundaries clearly and assertively communicate them to others. Doing this empowers you to safeguard your emotional and physical well-being, ensuring your needs are respected.

Seek support: Reach out to trusted friends, family members, or professionals who can supply guidance, understanding, and help with challenging situations. Having a support system in place can make a significant difference in how you feel.

Educate yourself: Continuously learn about healthy relationship dynamics. By gaining knowledge, you can better identify warning signs and make informed choices.

Consider professional help: If you have experienced mistreatment or abuse, seeking the support of a therapist or counselor can be instrumental in your healing process. They can provide the tools and guidance needed to overcome the effects of trauma and build a healthier future.

Bear in mind that by adopting proactive measures to safeguard your well-being, you can achieve a number of things:

1. You can prevent potential harm or distress by identifying and mitigating risks before they escalate.
2. You can foster a sense of personal empowerment and control over your life.
3. You can enhance your overall quality of life by supporting your physical health, mental resilience, and emotional stability.
4. You can create a safe and nurturing environment for yourself and those around you.

Next, we're going to shift our focus to some physical and emotional distress signals that we should never overlook. By understanding them, we can better equip ourselves to recognize and respond to situations that require immediate attention.

Chapter Ten
SYMPTOMS OF DISTRESS THAT SHOULD NOT BE IGNORED

Our bodies and minds are interconnected, and they each communicate with us through various means. Emotional signals may include feelings of sadness, anxiety, irritability, or a sense of overwhelm. Similarly, physical symptoms may manifest as headaches, sleep disturbances, changes in appetite, or unexplained aches and pains. These are not just mere discomforts; they are distress signals that our body and mind are sending us. We may tend to overlook these signs, prioritizing other things over our well-being, but *by understanding their importance and adopting proactive measures, we can empower ourselves.*

Physical and emotional symptoms of distress are our body's way of informing us that something is not right, and we need to pay attention. Just as the WEB method *helps in discerning whether someone will have a positive impac*t on your life, *your body's signals* can serve as a barometer for detecting adverse effects stemming from your interactions.

Remember, it's not selfish to prioritize your well-being, it's a necessary step towards a healthier and happier life. So, let's listen to our bodies and minds, understanding the signals they send us, and take appropriate action to care for ourselves.

"I had a friend who was going through a tough time but she always put on a brave face and insisted everything was fine. I started noticing some concerning signs like weight loss, constant fatigue, and withdrawal. I couldn't shake the feeling that something was wrong so I decided to reach out and express my concern and offer support. It turned out that she was struggling with severe anxiety and depression and I helped her get the professional help she needed. When someone tries to hide their suffering, it's important to pay attention to the signs and offer support." —Anonymous

EMOTIONAL WARNING SIGNS THAT YOU MAY EXPERIENCE

Our bodies often sense and respond to threats before our conscious minds can fully understand the situation. From subtle cues like a racing heartbeat or a knot in the stomach to more overt signs like trembling hands or a sudden surge of adrenaline, our body alerts us to potential threats.

Your intuition can often pick up subtle cues or warning signs that your conscious mind may not. Trust your instincts if you feel something is wrong.

When you're in a questionable situation, or around a person with toxic traits or a potentially dangerous person, ***there are several warning signs that your body, emotions, and intuition can use to alert you:***

Difficulty managing your temper: If you often get provoked to an angry explosion in your interactions, it may indicate that you're feeling significant stress, which is detrimental to your physical and mental health and unhealthy for those around you. Having difficulty controlling your anger may significantly affect others, particularly children. Consider counseling if you're frequently advised to calm down or control your temper.

If you're having difficulty controlling your temper, it could be a sign that you're experiencing strain within a relationship. According to registered nurse and professor Anie Kalayjian, individuals struggling with anger management issues often do not recognize the symptoms because *they feel fine when they are alone.* If a relationship is causing you to feel overpowering anger, it's crucial to find help from a professional who deals with anger management issues.

Feeling confused: When someone's behavior consistently leaves you confused and unsure of their intentions, it can instill a sense of unease and instability. Your confusion may stem from their mixed messages, inconsistent actions, or unclear communication. If you find yourself questioning someone's motives or intentions, or if their behavior consistently leaves you feeling confused and unsure of their intentions, it is a red flag.

Feeling drained or exhausted: People with toxic traits often leave us feeling emotionally drained or exhausted. If you feel depleted after interacting with someone, it may be that they negatively affect your well-being. (Warrior, 2023)

Feeling manipulated: Manipulation often involves tactics like guilt-tripping, gaslighting, or using emotional influence to get someone to do things. It is an unhealthy, harmful dynamic that can negatively impact your well-being, and it's important to address manipulation by maintaining boundaries When you feel coerced into doing something you don't want to do or feel uncomfortable doing, it's a sign that you're being manipulated.

Feeling hesitant or anxious: Feeling cautious or nervous around someone could indicate that your body and mind are signaling a potential threat. This could be due to a variety of reasons including past negative experiences, perceived negative intentions, or a feeling general sense of unease. These feelings serve as protective mechanisms to ensure your emotional and physical well-being.

Lowered self-esteem: If you consistently feel bad about yourself when you're around a certain someone, it can be a sign of a toxic dynamic. Decreased self-esteem can come from constant criticism, belittling, or undermining of your self-worth. It's essential to take note of this emotional impact and consider whether the relationship is good for you.

Memory problems: While memory issues can have various causes, relational stress and trauma can also affect your memory. If you find yourself experiencing a sudden onset of forgetfulness, it's a good idea to have a physical examination to rule out underlying medical conditions.

Mood swings and erratic behavior: Sometimes, we may not be aware of our emotional state, but the observations of others can supply valuable insight. If others express concern over changes to your disposition, mood, or behavior, it may be a sign that something is off and should be addressed.

BODY LANGUAGE: UNVEILING PHYSICAL WARNING SIGNS

If you find yourself in a potentially harmful or toxic scenario, you might experience physical symptoms like headaches, stomach discomfort, or muscle tension. Be mindful of any physical discomfort that you feel when you're in the presence of a certain individual or in a specific situation (Loryngalardi, 2021). It's crucial to heed these warning signs and take them seriously. If you feel threatened or suspect you're in a dangerous or toxic situation, prioritizing your safety and seeking assistance (if needed) is vital. If these feelings persist around a particular person, it might be time to reassess or end the relationship for your mental and physical well-being.

Avoiding social activity: If you find yourself avoiding social activities that you once enjoyed or prefer to stay at home rather than go out with friends, it could be a sign of a mental health challenge, or that you're going through a major life change, or experiencing high levels of stress. Sometimes it can be a sign of a physical health problem that is affecting your mood or energy levels. In any case, seek out a professional who can help.

Changes in eating patterns: A lack of appetite can indicate a disruption in your emotional well-being. When faced with stress, anxiety, or unhappiness, people may experience a loss of appetite, or conversely, engage in emotional eating as a coping mechanism. As mentioned in chapter two, changes in eating patterns can signal underlying issues that need to be addressed. A **loss of menstruation,** combined with an appetite change, is a warning sign possibly indicating a hormonal imbalance, or stress. Menstruation is a natural process regulated by hormones, and any disruption in this process, especially when combined with changes in appetite, should be taken seriously.

Chronic fatigue, tiredness, and lack of energy: When your mind is overwhelmed with emotional distress, it can take a toll on your body. As mentioned in chapter two, feeling constantly tired and lacking energy can be a sign that your body is struggling to cope with an emotional burden. Addressing these symptoms and seeking support to improve your overall well-being is a necessary step to return to wellness.

Compulsive/obsessive behaviors: If you engage in repetitive behaviors like hand washing, constant worrying, or performing rituals to feel safe or secure, or have intrusive thoughts that are challenging to control, it may be a sign of anxiety. It's essential to seek help if these behaviors interfere with your daily life.

Decreased sexual pleasure: If you're going through the motions of sex without feeling the pleasure you once did, it could be a sign that something needs to be addressed. It could be a sign of a physical health challenge or something else like depression, anxiety, or stress. Furthermore, it could indicate relationship concerns like lack of emotional intimacy or unresolved conflicts. It's important to communicate openly about these matters and seek professional help if needed. A physical checkup can help rule out any underlying medical concerns.

Increased heart rate or feelings of unease: Your body may react to danger by increasing your heart rate or making you feel nervous, anxious, or on edge. Feeling uneasy or jumpy around someone could indicate something is off. This discomfort may stem from a lack of trust in them, unresolved conflicts between you, or a general feeling of unease when you're around them. It's important to pay attention to these feelings and consider whether they indicate that you feel unsafe. (Booz, 2023)

Sleep disturbances: If you're experiencing changes in your sleep patterns, such as sleeping more or less than usual, have difficulty falling asleep, or find yourself waking up in the middle of the night and struggling to go back to sleep, it could be a sign of emotional distress, according to Dr. Goodstein, a clinical professor of psychiatry at NYU Medical Center. Recurring sleep disturbances without any physical reasons found by your doctor may be linked to anxiety or depression.

Unexplained physical symptoms: If you have physical complaints that cannot be explained despite a thorough medical examination, it could be a sign that your body is expressing emotional distress. Common physical concerns that are linked to emotional distress include headaches, stomach issues, diarrhea, constipation, and chronic pain, particularly backaches.

Weight fluctuations: If you've noticed a significant gain or loss of weight without any changes in your diet or exercise routine, it could be a sign of something requiring a closer look. As mentioned previously in chapter three, a constant preoccupation with food, weight, and body image may indicate an eating disorder says Abby Aronowitz, Ph.D., director of SelfHelpDirectives.com. Consult a healthcare professional if such changes are seen, as they can supply a proper diagnosis and treatment plan.

It's interesting to note that doctors say that these signs can all be a normal part of the human condition. Goodstein states that the presence of anxiety, depressed mood, or mental conflicts *does not* necessarily mean there's a problem, because these qualities are part of the human experience. But if you find yourself constantly on high alert, something may be going on that needs a closer look. According to Aronowitz, the frequency, intensity, and duration of distress are essential factors in figuring out the seriousness of any situation.

An awareness of these physical and emotional symptoms can serve to protect you from their long-term impact. If you're experiencing any of the symptoms mentioned, it's crucial to discuss your concerns with your doctor, who can provide a comprehensive evaluation. Seeking help and support is a brave step towards relieving your symptoms and improving your well-being. Please remember you're not alone; there are people who care and want to help you. Making informed decisions about your relationships and prioritizing your safety and well-being are essential for a healthy and fulfilling life (WebMD Contributors, 2022).

Chapter Eleven
HIDDEN WOUNDS: THE COMPLEXITIES OF TRAUMA

It's not surprising to hear that personal traumatic experiences can have a significant impact on relationships. Trauma can affect how individuals communicate, trust, and connect with others, and can lead to difficulties in forming and keeping healthy relationships. When an individual undergoes a traumatic experience, it can provoke emotional "triggers," which are stimuli or events that act as reminders of the traumatic incident. It's important to note that these emotional hotspots vary from person to person, as trauma affects each of us in unique ways.

Experiencing trauma may heighten our emotional responses, and increase feelings of anxiety, fear, and anger. Our sensitive areas can feel intense and overwhelming sometimes, and our reactions to them can be automatic and involuntary, making it challenging to manage our emotions when we're in touchy situations.

By recognizing and validating each other's sensitive areas, we can work together to create a safe and supportive environment for everyone.

THE IMPACT OF TRAUMATIC STRESS

According to the American Psychiatric Association, it is estimated that 7 out of 100 people in the United States will be diagnosed with Post-Traumatic Stress Disorder (PTSD) at some point in their lives. PTSD is a mental health challenge caused by exposure to incredibly stressful events like natural disasters, accidents, assault, terrorist events, war, loss of a loved one, illness diagnosis, hospitalization, and seeing violence. For many, this event was a singular traumatic occurrence.

"I knew someone who experienced a traumatic event in their past. She would often have nightmares and flashbacks, reliving the event. She had difficulty sleeping and was easily startled. She avoided certain places and sometimes had intense emotional reactions. It was clear that she was still deeply affected by the trauma and needed my support." —Anonymous

Common symptoms of PTSD include intrusive thoughts, nightmares, flashbacks, or physical reactions when reminded of the event, avoidance, changes in thoughts or mood, feeling detached, estranged, or numb, difficulty sleeping or concentrating, irritability, intense anger, hypervigilance, self-harming, feeling on-edge, and depression.

Women suffering from childhood related PTSD may experience added challenges with thinking clearly (Gattuso, 2018). It's important to note that not everyone with PTSD experiences all symptoms and the severity and their duration can vary.

For survivors of *ongoing trauma*, like emotional abuse, gaslighting, neglect, or coercive control, PTSD symptoms can be particularly intense, and may indicate a *different form of PTSD* called Complex Post-Traumatic Stress Disorder (C-PTSD), which is a relatively new term in the realm of emotional wellness. Complex Post-Traumatic Stress Disorder was officially recognized in 2013 as a "trauma and stress-related disorder."

THE LONG-TERM EFFECTS OF C-PTSD ON EMOTIONAL WELL-BEING

C-PTSD is distinct from PTSD as it arises from the accumulation of multiple or prolonged traumatic events rather than a singular incident. Individuals affected by C-PTSD experience PTSD symptoms but because of the repeated exposure to trauma such as ongoing emotional abuse, living in an unpredictable environment, continual fear of abandonment, constant hypervigilance, persistent gaslighting, and ongoing coercive control, they experience additional symptoms.

EMOTIONAL WOUNDS: RECOGNIZING AND TACKLING THE HOT SPOTS

People working through C-PTSD may experience:

- feelings of shame or guilt

- feelings of responsibility for the traumatic events

- difficulty controlling emotions

- a loss of attention and focus

- feeling isolated from friends and family

- relationship difficulties

- destructive or risky behavior

- suicidal thoughts

- ongoing worry

- adrenal burnout

- chronic inflammatory disorders

- mental and physical exhaustion

- anxiety

- weight loss or gain

- self-gaslighting

It is crucial to note that children who have endured neglect or mistreatment are susceptible to developing C-PTSD, and as they transition into adulthood, may face an elevated risk of physical illness and revictimization.

People who have experienced complex trauma may show a heightened sensitivity to specific emotional areas, which can make navigating life more challenging. It is important to approach someone's emotional sensitivities with empathy and understanding. To effectively support individuals who have experienced trauma, it is crucial to create a secure and affirming environment combined with plenty of active listening, empathy, and patience. By recognizing and affirming someone's experiences, we foster a nurturing atmosphere that promotes healing and personal growth.

When you focus on the hurt, you continue to suffer.

NAVIGATING LIFE: HOW EMOTIONAL TRIGGERS IMPACT RELATIONSHIPS

In order to gain a deeper understanding of C-PTSD, it is necessary to recognize that our emotional hotspots or sensitivities act as warning signals for potential danger or threats. They can become automatic reactions that make it challenging to navigate daily life and relationships.

These triggers can be wounds that still need healing, or they may be unrealistic expectations that serve as hotspots. It's essential to understand and take responsibility for our emotional sensitivities. By identifying them we may gain a better understanding of our feelings and reactions. This self-awareness can help us develop strategies to manage emotions more effectively, and although we may not be aware of all of our hotspots, it is possible to cultivate healthy responses to those we're aware of. The simple *awareness that a hotspot has been activated* can sometimes be enough to keep our reactions in check. (Franco, 2018)

By recognizing our sensitive areas, we can address the underlying issues that may be contributing to them, leading to personal growth and improved emotional well-being.

Chapter Twelve
NARCISSISM AWARENESS GRIEF: AN EMOTIONAL ROLLERCOASTER

Narcissism is a complex personality disorder involving an inflated sense of self-importance, constant need for approval, powerful sense of entitlement, and a profound lack of empathy. Since it is a spectrum disorder, people can have narcissistic traits without having diagnosable narcissism personality disorder. These people typically seek admiration and take advantage of others for their own gain. Additionally, they have difficulty recognizing and valuing the feelings and needs of others. They may manipulate and exploit others without remorse, and *their relationships often suffer*.

It is important to note that if someone has narcissistic traits, it *does not* necessarily mean that they have narcissistic personality disorder (NPD). People can show narcissistic traits to varying degrees *without* having diagnosable NPD because narcissism exists on a spectrum.

While it is true that narcissistic personality disorder can be challenging to treat, it is inaccurate to say that people with NPD can't be helped with therapy. (Keohan, 2023) Most people with NPD symptoms don't pursue therapy. They blame others for problems, which can make it difficult for them to recognize a need for treatment, and their belief in their superiority may cause resistance to the idea of taking responsibility for their actions. Additionally, they may lack insight into the impact of their behavior, not recognizing it as problematic.

"I once went on a date with someone who seemed perfect in their dating profile. They were charming, successful, and had all the right qualities. But as the evening progressed, I noticed he would constantly interrupt me and steer the conversation back to himself. It was like I was talking to myself! This behavior was a clear red flag for narcissism and it made me realize the importance of paying attention to how someone treats others."
—*Anonymous*

When a person with NPD decides to seek treatment, it can be challenging for any therapy to be effective because of the ingrained and deep-seated patterns of thinking and behavior that need changing. Shifting these patterns requires a great deal of self-reflection, introspection, and the willingness to take responsibility for one's actions. If someone struggles with these, it may hinder any therapy's effectiveness. Profound change requires strong motivation and a willingness to engage in the process.

One specific approach that has been shown to be beneficial is called schema therapy, (Hudson, 2023) which focuses on finding and changing deeply ingrained patterns of thinking and behavior. Humanistic therapy, solution-focused brief therapy, narrative therapy, and mindfulness-based therapy have also been found to be effective. (Guam 2023). Other beneficial approaches include cognitive-behavioral therapy, transference-focused psychotherapy, mentalization-based therapy, dialectical behavior therapy, eye movement desensitization and reprocessing therapy and metacognitive interpersonal therapy. Each of these methods requires a commitment to the process and a willingness to explore one's underlying emotional hotspots.

Therapists may want to work with the narcissistic individual's family or close friends to create a more complete treatment plan. It's crucial for all parties to manage their expectations, because while total transformation may not be feasible, it is possible for the individual to learn more adaptive coping styles, which may lead to improved relationships.

HEALING FROM NARCISSISTIC RELATIONSHIPS: AN EMOTIONAL JOURNEY

When we recognize someone's narcissistic traits, acknowledging that this person is primarily focused on themselves, lacks empathy, and manipulates others, including us, for their own gain, it may spark a specific type of grief process to begin unfolding within us.

Narcissism Awareness Grief is not a clinical diagnosis, but a *term* coined by Dr. Christine Hammond. It describes the emotional and psychological process we go through after becoming aware that we are in a relationship with someone who has narcissistic traits.

If you're feeling narcissism awareness grief, you may have felt a strange sense of relief when you discovered that the drama and trauma you've endured has a name. You may have felt a rush of validation as you understood that you're not alone, that you're not "crazy," and that you haven't imagined any of it. Narcissistic trauma and abuse are *real things*, and you *can recover* from them.

"Whatever the situation may be, to fully achieve peace within yourself, it is necessary for those who have been victims of narcissistic personalities to complete all the stages of acceptance and learn to grow beyond their previously fabricated reality."
—*Christine Hammond*

I have vivid memories of my own experience with NAG. As I gradually became aware of a loved one's narcissistic traits, I was overwhelmed with feelings of denial, disbelief, resentment, and a profound sadness that kept me fixated on past hurts. To start my healing process, I realized that I needed to dive deep into each stage of my grief and allow myself to explore unthinkable thoughts and experience intensely painful emotions. Only afterward could I begin to explore the idea of Acceptance and move forward into recovery.

Navigating narcissism awareness grief requires patience and a willingness to give oneself over to the process, gifting oneself the time to allow each step to unfold organically. A support system including a professional therapist and emotionally stable friends and family can be highly beneficial during this period because NAG can be a complex and challenging experience. We may relentlessly question ourselves as we struggle to process and reframe our experiences using our new insights.

Narcissism awareness grief can significantly impact us physically, emotionally, and mentally. We may experience physical symptoms such as fatigue, appetite changes, difficulty sleeping, and even physical pain. Emotionally, we may encounter intense feelings of denial, anger, sadness, betrayal, and a deep sense of loss for the relationship that we *thought* we had. Mentally, we may struggle with self-doubt, low self-esteem, and difficulty trusting others. It's important to note that these effects will vary from person to person, as everyone's experience with NAG is unique.

TRANSFORMING PAIN INTO PERSONAL GROWTH

Like the well-known Kubler-Ross model of the 'five stages of grief,' the process of narcissism awareness grief involves multiple stages, with an added and crucial phase known as "Rewriting." This stage serves as a catalyst for profound healing to begin. Narcissism awareness grief is not linear, its phases are not experienced in any particular order. We can go back and forth among them throughout the process.

It's worth mentioning that to reach the stage of Acceptance, it's necessary to progress through all the other stages. Since it *is* possible to get stuck and remain stuck in any stage, if you find yourself in this situation, it's vital to find help and support to continue moving forward.

Be willing to lose someone's approval in order to gain your own.

THE SIX STAGES OF NARCISSISM AWARENESS GRIEF

To provide a clearer understanding of narcissism awareness grief, we'll dive into the specific traits of each stage. They include:

1. **Denial:** As you ponder the likelihood of someone falling within the narcissism spectrum it could be unsettling for you. Even if you're confident that they are affected, you might downplay the impact of their behavior until you reach a point where you can no longer ignore it. At that moment, you'll become aware of the scope of the issue and its impact on you and others. This marks your entry into narcissism awareness grief.

2. **Anger:** It's common to experience a deep sense of "righteous indignation," a natural response to mistreatment or abuse. It's completely understandable to feel intense anger, which can serve as a powerful motivator, and a driving force for positive change.

3. **Bargaining:** It's completely understandable to wish for a different kind of relationship and to question why you didn't notice the narcissistic traits earlier. It's important to remember that finding clear answers to these questions may not always be possible. It's common to experience a deep sense of loss and sadness, and you might adopt similar behaviors as the narcissistic individual, questioning the validity of your thoughts and feelings. Try to be aware of this and as gentle and compassionate as you can with yourself during this time.

4. **Depression:** When you understand that you cannot change the person affected or make them see you differently, a deep sadness may set in. If you adopted their limited and incorrect beliefs about yourself, you may have missed out on opportunities, and your relationships may have suffered. Accepting that this person cannot see you as an individual in your own right, or feel remorse, or apologize to you can be a heavy burden to bear. You may feel overwhelmed at the amount of work ahead of you to reconcile your past and heal, knowing that they will feel no accountability or responsibility whatsoever.

5. **Rewriting:** Significant healing opportunities await you in this phase. Here you will begin re-writing your narrative with courage and self-love. You may also begin accepting that you have no control over someone's narcissistic traits and how this person perceives you. You'll start to apply new insights to your present *and past* interactions. You may recognize that by internalizing their faulty perspectives of you, it has impacted your life in some

negative ways. Additionally, you may realize that their hurtful behavior has *nothing to do with you and never did.*

By updating your historical view of yourself with new insight, you may undergo a transformative process, discovering your lovability, prioritizing your self-care, and feeling worthy of keeping personal boundaries, potentially leading to one of the happiest times of your life.

6. **Acceptance:** As you progress through the stages, Acceptance becomes more natural and effortless. As you recognize someone's narcissistic traits, you may experience a brand-new sense of freedom in realizing that you are not responsible for, nor are you capable of, changing this individual. It can be such a relief to let go and move forward! Now, you can anticipate their behavior and take action to make interactions with them feel safer or more tolerable. Alternatively, you have the choice to end all contact. You'll come to understand that these choices are yours alone and are independent of their desires or expectations. Feeling a newfound sense of self-empowerment, autonomy, self-efficacy, and inner peace may be beyond what you ever thought possible.

FINDING STRENGTH IN VULNERABILITY: THE PATH TO RECOVERY AND SELF-DISCOVERY

If you are experiencing narcissism awareness grief, it is essential to prioritize your self-care and seek support from trusted friends, family, or professionals. Here are some other steps you can take:

1. Acknowledge and validate your feelings: It is crucial to recognize and accept all your feelings. Validating your emotions is a significant step in the healing process.

2. Educate yourself: Learning about narcissism and its adverse effects may provide you with a better understanding of your experiences. Accurate information can empower you to make informed decisions and take necessary recovery steps.

3. Set up boundaries: Setting clear limits can help you protect your physical and emotional well-being. This may involve limiting contact, asserting personal needs, and refusing to engage with anyone who uses manipulative behaviors like gaslighting.

4. Seek professional help: Consulting with a therapist or counselor specializing in narcissistic abuse or trauma can be beneficial. They can provide guidance, support, and strategies for coping with narcissism awareness grief.

5. Practice self-care: Engaging in activities that promote self-care and self-compassion includes physical exercise, meditation, journaling, spending time with friends and loved ones, and pursuing hobbies and interests, all of which may bring you peace and joy.

6. Build a support network: Surround yourself with understanding, empathetic individuals who provide a sense of validation and support. Joining support groups or joining online communities may help you connect with others sharing similar experiences. *Please scrutinize these groups carefully to ensure that they are appropriately moderated and secured.*

As you use this new way to see and understand the narcissistic individual, you may realize that there is nothing, and there never was anything inherently wrong with or lacking within you, as they may have wanted you to believe.

Chapter Thirteen
THE DARK SIDE OF CONSTANTLY PUTTING OTHERS FIRST

In today's interconnected world, many of us may find ourselves caught in the trap of people-pleasing and codependency.

People-pleasing refers to the tendency to prioritize the needs and desires of others above our own, often at the expense of our own well-being. It involves seeking approval and validation from others, and feeling a deep sense of anxiety or guilt when we are unable to meet their expectations.

While codependency can involve people-pleasing tendencies, not all people-pleasers are necessarily codependent. Codependency, simply put, is the process of losing oneself for the sake of helping another. It involves a more complex and deeply rooted pattern of behavior. As Robert Subby describes in his book "Lost in the Shuffle: The Co-Dependent Reality," it can feel like erasing parts of our identity, and sacrificing the very essence of what defines us, as we strive to make others happy, and conform to their expectations of who we should be. Codependent individuals prioritize other's life experiences, happiness, and fulfillment at the expense of their own. It's most detrimental outcome is a ***lost sense of self***, the feeling of existing as a shadow of one's former self.

Codependency is made of unhealthy behavior patterns, and it often develops in relationships where someone relies on another for emotional support. If we became codependent as children, we may have been someone's emotional or physical caretaker, required to mature quickly and take responsibilities that were not ours or were not age appropriate. If we're struggling with codependency, we've likely become adept at noticing the moods and behavioral patterns of others, and we've honed the ability to predict their actions, and we've probably become accustomed to taking responsibilities that rightfully belong to them.

Both people-pleasing and codependency can have profound impacts on our mental and emotional well-being. People-pleasing and codependent dynamics can hinder personal growth and result in a lack of autonomy and independence, leading to further enabling, dependency, and relationship imbalances. It is important to understand and address these patterns in order to cultivate healthier and more fulfilling relationships.

THE JOURNEY OF A LOST SELF

The concept of codependency was developed by Melody Beattie, an American author and self-help counselor, introducing the idea in her book "Codependent No More" published in 1986.

Codependency progresses through three stages, ranging from mild to severe. Like any other physical and mental health concern, it may vary in severity and intensity, with individuals falling at different points along the spectrum.

Beattie describes the three stages of codependency as:

The Caretaker: In this early stage, you may notice that you're paying more attention to someone to gain their approval or make them happy. You may neglect your needs, plans, goals, and boundaries to accommodate this individual. You may check their moods, becoming hypervigilant, feeling a strong need to please them or keep them calm. Denying and rationalizing their problem behaviors and creating explanations that maintain a sense of safety for yourself are common occurrences. As a caretaker, you may endure gaslighting and actively avoid situations that could lead to disagreements.

The Loser: Codependent behaviors become more ingrained, and we become overly focused on other's needs. We neglect our own well-being and feel anxious, guilty, or ashamed. We may withdraw from other relationships and activities we enjoy. Our self-esteem decreases, and we *continue compromising ourselves for the sake of the relationship, or* to maintain a sense of stability. Our focus becomes taking their "emotional temperature" and checking their moods, as we adjust our behavior and expectations according to what we sense is happening with them. We may feel angry, disappointed, unloved, or unimportant, and in an effort to feel better we may use harmful coping styles like over-eating, starving, binging, physical self-harming, compulsive buying, gambling,

THE DARK SIDE OF CONSTANTLY PUTTING OTHERS FIRST

stealing, engaging in risky sexual activity, and abusing substances; anything that helps us deal with our emotional pain.

The Martyr: As our codependency becomes profoundly entrenched, we may feel trapped and experience a range of adverse effects on our mental and emotional well-being. We may suffer health issues like stomachaches, nightmares, headaches, muscle pain, tension, and jaw clenching. Self-esteem and self-care are almost nonexistent, replaced by feelings of hopelessness, helplessness, anger, resentment, and unhappiness. Codependent adults spend much of their time thinking about how to satisfy and make life better for another while at the same time, their own social, professional, and personal responsibilities are neglected despite the problems this creates.

"I remember a friend who was always putting others' needs before her own. She would constantly go out of her way to make everyone happy, even if it meant sacrificing plans she had made or activities she enjoyed. She often felt overwhelmed and exhausted from constantly trying to please others. This codependent behavior took a toll on her mental and emotional health." —Anonymous

It's important to note that these stages are not universally experienced in the same order or intensity by everyone, as codependency manifests differently for each of us.

SELF-SACRIFICING BEHAVIOR AND THE NEED TO BE NEEDED

When we're codependent, we feel responsible for people and problems that are not our responsibility, yet if we don't try to help, fix, or control, we often feel guilty or ashamed. It feels *wrong* not to jump in, take charge, or help others who seem to be struggling, even when they *haven't* asked for help or reached out for assistance. We feel it's our job to take action, take over, and fix because helping and fixing other people's problems feels good and gives us *a sense of purpose.*

If we're codependent, we most likely don't have boundaries; if we do, we don't enforce them. We often share too much information and still assume we're doubted. We explain and overexplain. We seek affirmation (which can look like neediness, clinginess, or insecurity) from others to feel "good enough" and know that we matter to someone. We tend to make excuses and justify other's poor behavior. We internalize their blame and downplay or ignore the pain they inflict upon us. We gaslight ourselves about the motives behind their mistreatment and convince ourselves that it's acceptable for them to continue.

Are you using codependent behavior? To see if you are, answer the following questions. In this context, "someone" refers to **a non-disabled, mentally competent adult:**

- Do you engage in actions that prevent someone from experiencing the consequences of their choices?

THE DARK SIDE OF CONSTANTLY PUTTING OTHERS FIRST

- Do you assume responsibility for someone's actions or poor decisions?

When you take responsibility (or accept blame or make excuses) for someone's behavior, it enables them to continue because (a) you have removed all responsibility from them and placed it on yourself, and (b) there are no negative consequences for them, thus, no lesson is learned. This cycle reinforces irresponsibility and fosters a sense of entitlement.

- Do you do things for someone that they could do for themselves?
- Are you preoccupied or concerned with someone's life or choices?
- Do you place a lower priority on your needs or responsibilities than you do on someone else's?
- Are you attracted to someone who is emotionally or physically unavailable?
- Do you believe you must be in a romantic relationship for life to be meaningful?
- Are you trying to control someone's behavior or choices?
- Does it feel impossible to end an unsatisfying or hurtful relationship?
- Do you resent helping someone and not getting any thanks for it?
- Have you stopped taking time for yourself to do something that you enjoy?
- Have you begun to de-value your self-care?

- Do you fear for someone's safety but are willing to risk your own?
- Are you shielding someone from the consequences of their actions?
- Do you take responsibility for how someone is feeling?
- Do you take responsibility for someone's actions?
- Are you trying to fix someone's problems when they haven't asked you to?
- Are you helping or rescuing because it makes you feel better when you try to control what happens next?
- Do you feel like your life is full of unwanted drama?
- Do you manage or control someone's life?
- Have you been called "controlling" or a "control freak?"
- Do you clean up someone's messes, both figuratively and otherwise?

Dropping our codependent traits can be challenging. To be successful, we must delve into our relationships to understand the dynamics at play. Personally, when I was ready for the challenge, I embarked on this journey by examining how I spent my time and who benefited from it. I started recognizing instances where I prioritized others' needs while neglecting my own. I questioned the reasons behind these choices and gradually became more aware of my thoughts and decision-making process. I also became aware of my negative self-talk and the belief that I had to prioritize everyone else's needs above mine. To make positive changes, I actively worked on improving my thoughts and self-talk, and I surrounded myself with

THE DARK SIDE OF CONSTANTLY PUTTING OTHERS FIRST

supportive, emotionally healthy friends, and let go of those who were not.

My hardest lesson was learning to let go of the desire to control outcomes. I eventually realized that when people are shielded from the natural consequences of their actions, they struggle to take responsibility, develop social skills, and cultivate the necessary qualities for successful relationships, like sharing, honesty, listening, negotiation, and compromise.

Throughout my journey, I discovered the importance of self-reflection, intention, making conscious choices, and surrounding myself with a supportive network. Letting go of control and allowing others to experience the consequences of their actions has been a slow, deliberate, and sometimes painful process that has become a transformative experience.

If you're so inclined, you could begin reducing your codependent tendencies by supporting others in a manner that encourages their personal growth and development, without enabling or rescuing them from the consequences of their choices or behavior. It means becoming comfortable with allowing others the dignity of making and learning from their mistakes. Understanding that your self-sacrificing behavior may have negative consequences is essential because sometimes, being helpful can hinder someone's progress or growth. Instead of rescuing, try letting go of the need to control and set some boundaries instead. Notice how that feels. Are you able to find comfort, freedom, and peace in doing that? Are you filled with unease, worry, or tension, unable to let go? Devoting time to reflect on these questions can promote valuable self-awareness and find areas to work on for your personal growth.

Here's the thing: individuals with toxic traits are often drawn to those who struggle with codependent tendencies. This attraction makes sense when you consider the dynamics at play. If you suspect that you have some codependent traits, it's crucial to address and eliminate these tendencies to reduce your appeal to unsupportive, non-nurturing, self-centered individuals.

Try engaging in practices to regain your sense of self-identity and set up healthier boundaries in your relationships. Healing codependency involves self-awareness, self-reflection, intention, and support. Here are some steps to take to begin your healing journey:

1. Recognize and acknowledge your codependent patterns: Become aware of your codependent behaviors. This may involve reflecting on your relationships and finding unhealthy dynamics or patterns of enabling, rescuing, or sacrificing your own needs for others.

2. Educate yourself: Learning about codependency can help you understand its subtleties and underlying causes. Many books, articles, and online resources are available that supply valuable insights and strategies.

3. Seek help: Contact a therapist or counselor specializing in codependency. They can provide guidance, support, and tools to help you address any underlying matters or traumas contributing to your codependency.

4. Join a support group: Connecting with others with similar experiences can be incredibly helpful. Joining a support group or attending Codependents Anonymous (CoDA) meetings may provide a safe space to share your struggles, gain support, and learn from others on a similar journey.

5. Practice self-care and self-compassion: Prioritize your well-being and practice activities that nurture your physical, emotional, spiritual, and mental health. This could mean setting boundaries, engaging in enjoyable activities, practicing mindfulness or meditation, and seeking healthy outlets for stress and emotions.

6. Challenge negative beliefs and patterns: Codependency often stems from deep-rooted beliefs and thinking patterns. Challenge these and begin replacing them with healthier, more empowering ones by working with a therapist or using self-help techniques.

7. Build new relationships: Create healthy, balanced relationships as you heal from codependency. Surround yourself with supportive and emotionally healthy people who respect your boundaries and encourage your personal growth. Let go of those who do not.

You can stop people-pleasing and begin healing codependent traits by embarking on a path of self-discovery and reinvention. You can regain self-confidence, cultivate healthy self-esteem, attract mentally balanced individuals, and create fulfilling relationships. With patience, persistence, and practice, you can move forward to embracing a rich and satisfying life.

It's a process, not an event.

Chapter Fourteen
PROTECTING OURSELVES: TAKING CRUCIAL STEPS

A lack of boundaries invites a lack of respect.

In our pursuit of love, validation, and affection, the fear of losing someone's approval can trap us in a never-ending cycle of people-pleasing, emotional suffering, resentment, and unhappiness. But by setting up boundaries, we can liberate ourselves from this destructive pattern. When we set and enforce boundaries, we establish a solid base of mutual respect, self-care, and realistic expectations. This chapter delves into the significance of setting limits and how doing so empowers us to create more satisfying relationships while prioritizing our well-being.

Here's the thing: WE get to determine what's acceptable to us and what's not. By setting clear limits, we empower ourselves to prioritize our needs.

What you allow is what will continue.

Protecting ourselves from mistreatment requires several actions, including setting clear and firm limits with others, developing strong self-esteem, recognizing our value, and understanding that we deserve to be treated with respect and kindness. It requires that we clearly communicate our expectations and possibly seek support from trusted friends, family, or professionals who can provide guidance. Protecting ourselves requires a commitment to ourselves and a *willingness to prioritize* our needs and safety.

FINDING FREEDOM BY SETTING LIMITS

Contrary to what some believe, boundaries are not "putting up a wall." They are not a threat or a manipulation, and enforcing boundaries is not a form of coercive control.

Instead, a boundary is our "line in the sand" that is not to be crossed. It means you've thought about someone's behaviors that are acceptable to you and those that are not, and you have set limits around the ones that are not. Boundaries are factual, not emotional.

Strange things can happen when we don't have boundaries in place; we might find ourselves denying our own emotions or engaging in actions that are not in our best interest in an attempt to gain someone's love, approval, or acceptance. We may allow hurtful behavior to continue and blame ourselves for a perceived weakness when all we need are some healthy boundaries.

We need them to keep from living in a cycle of regret or feeling resentful and used. Setting and enforcing boundaries is an act of self-respect and a form of self-care and self-empowerment. Anna Taylor said it best: "Love yourself enough to set boundaries. Your time and energy are precious. You get to choose how you use it. You teach people how to treat you by deciding what you will and won't accept." It can feel scary because sometimes the stakes feel high.

"I remember a time when my sister and I were living together. We had always been close, but there were times when she borrowed my clothes without asking and did not return them for weeks, and it really started to bother me. I decided it was time for a boundary. I explained how I felt about her borrowing my clothes without my permission. We came up with a system where she would ask for permission first, and we set up a timeframe for returning the items. We both felt heard and understood, and it strengthened our relationship." —Anonymous

Without clear boundaries, we may find ourselves prioritizing the needs and desires of others over our own or feeling obligated to say yes to every request or demand. Additionally, neglecting our needs may lead to negative consequences for our physical and emotional health. As mentioned previously in chapter fourteen, we may eventually become depleted and overwhelmed by constantly putting others before ourselves. Establishing and maintaining healthy boundaries allows us to prioritize our safety, emotional stability, and mental health, ensuring that we care for ourselves while continuing our relationships with others.

PROTECTING OURSELVES: TAKING CRUCIAL STEPS

EMPOWERING YOURSELF: CHOOSING TO DRAW THE LINE

For individuals struggling with people-pleasing or codependency, learning to say "no" can be challenging. If we're in a people-pleasing or codependent relationship, we'll find ourselves saying yes when we want to say no and feeling resentful and angry for doing the opposite of what we want. The desire to be liked, loved, and needed is a natural human tendency, and understandably, we may fear losing those.

The word "no" is a boundary. "No" is a choice. "No" is a complete sentence. Saying "No, I won't do that" or "I will no longer _____" is a way to honor our true feelings. It's an affirmation of our integrity and beliefs.

Saying what we mean and meaning what we say is a courageous act of strength and faith in ourselves.

I've heard that it's far better to use an assertive no than a submissive yes. We can say no with love and compassion. It doesn't have to feel meanspirited. Your yes will be stronger and more meaningful if you say no now and then.

Setting a boundary requires three things:

1. Acknowledge that you have a specific physical or emotional need that affects your happiness, emotional or physical well-being, or sense of safety.
2. Observe someone's *behavior* that directly challenges this need.
3. Set the consequences for the behavior. You will take this *action* when that behavior shows up. (When that line is crossed, you will need to know ahead of time what you will do and be prepared to do it.)

Make sure that you will be able to carry out the consequence. When we don't enforce our boundaries, we convey that we're not serious and can end up feeling defeated or resentful. If you don't feel you can realistically carry out the consequence, you need to create a new one.

HONORING AUTHENTICITY AND NURTURING HEALTHY CONNECTIONS

What do you need to feel safe, loved, secure, happy, rested, and mentally healthy? This question can be challenging, so take the time to dive into it. Here are some considerations: Do you require an earlier bedtime than your partner? Do you need daily quiet time away from your children for personal reasons? Are there any specific medications or supplements that you need? Do you need to incorporate or avoid particular foods in your diet? Is there something that someone says or does that makes you uncomfortable? Does someone's behavior make you feel emotionally or physically unsafe? Does someone consistently disrespect you, show contempt or say hurtful things? Reflect on people or situations you would avoid if given the choice and ask yourself why. If you could change something, what would it be? Your answer might be, "I want them to stop doing _____" or "I'd like it if they did _____."

It would be great if they did what we wanted, but because we cannot control other people's thoughts or actions, we must reframe our approach. We cannot force someone to stop their actions or change how they treat us, but we do not have to accept unacceptable behavior. We can alter *our response* to their behavior. *We can change the outcome for ourselves*.

For example:

Identify a need: *I need to feel safe.*

Identify someone's behavior that directly challenges this need: *I feel unsafe as a passenger when they drink and drive.*

Identify the action you will take when this behavior shows up. This is the consequence: *I will call a friend, a taxi, or a rideshare or make another choice that protects or removes me from the situation.*

Now put it all together to create the boundary: I need to feel safe. I feel unsafe as a passenger when they drink and drive. When they choose to drink and drive, I will call a friend, a taxi, or a rideshare or make another choice that protects or removes me from the situation.

Only you can determine your boundaries because **no one knows what's best for you but you.** You don't need someone's permission to set a boundary, and you don't need them to approve, allow, or agree to it. Boundaries are not about anyone but you. They are created by you, for you, to take care of only you.

Know who deserves an explanation, who deserves an answer, and who deserves nothing at all.

If you choose to inform someone about a new boundary, you should thoroughly understand your motivation. Choose the best time, and state only the facts (keep it unemotional.) You do not need to justify, answer questions, or deal with drama. As uncomfortable as it might be to say and enforce a boundary, you may want to do it as a way *to express your expectations*. You could say something like: "I need to feel safe when you drive (the unmet need), and I don't feel safe when you drink and drive. In the future, if you decide to drink and drive, I will contact a friend, or call a taxi or a rideshare." This straightforward approach does not involve drama, explaining, apologizing, waiting for agreement or approval, or seeking acceptance.

Do not inform someone of a new boundary if you think they will intentionally break it to test you. ***Do not inform*** them if it could provoke an argument or endanger you. They will eventually learn that the boundary exists when you enforce it by carrying out the consequences.

Ask Yourself:

Does the boundary take care of me? Am I trying to control this person's behavior, or am I trying to take care of myself? Is my boundary more of an ultimatum or a threat? A healthy boundary allows others to make choices, *including the choice to do the thing you don't want them to do.* If there is no choice or only one "choice," then it's more of an ultimatum or a threat, and you need to tweak it. Do you see the difference between trying to control someone's behavior and setting a boundary to take care of yourself?

By setting boundaries, we can define what is acceptable and what is not to ensure that our needs and well-being are prioritized. I think of boundaries as a form of self-care that help us maintain our authenticity.

There may be instances where someone in our lives becomes hurtful, critical, or judgmental towards us as we establish and enforce boundaries. They don't like our new boundary, and that's OK. To prepare for negative reactions, consider developing strategies to remain calm and assertive, communicate openly and honestly, and express empathy for their feelings. Stay firm and seek support from trusted friends or professionals if needed. You've got this.

PART IV:
HEALING FROM RELATIONAL TRAUMA

Content Warning:

This section contains frank discussions of relationship red flags, mental health challenges, and other sensitive topics including neglect and abuse. Please be aware that reading about these issues may be difficult for some readers.

Reader discretion is advised.

Diane Metcalf
168 • Red Flags: Icks, Personality Quirks, or Warning Signs? How to Know the Difference

Chapter Fifteen
THE IMPACT OF SHAME

The shame of enduring mistreatment or abuse can leave long-lasting scars.

Shaming is a control tactic used by people with toxic tendencies. It's often accomplished through the use of mixed messages, sarcasm, scapegoating, narcissistic rages, gaslighting, and trauma bonding. Individuals with toxic traits may shame others to keep their sense of superiority and minimize future threats to their image. By eroding *our* self-esteem and self-confidence, they reinforce their own "untouchable" status. Shame undermines our self-worth and instills a sense of inadequacy. Our feelings of shame convince us that we are unworthy of acceptance or belonging, and instead deserve criticism, rejection, and loneliness.

The reasons for shaming can vary, but they all enhance an individual's sense of power while diminishing our enjoyment of life.

EMBRACING VULNERABILITY: THE PATH TO HEALING SHAME

The term "abuse" is often linked to shame, especially in the context of relationships. Many of us downplay certain painful experiences because we hesitate to label our loved ones as "abusers," or ourselves as victims for that matter. However, this reluctance serves only to intensify feelings of shame and contribute to a negative self-image, leading to unfavorable comparisons of ourselves with our peers.

"I knew a couple where one partner would frequently use shaming to control the other. She would belittle her partner in front of others, criticize his appearance or abilities, and make him feel inadequate. It was heartbreaking to witness the emotional toll it took on him." —Anonymous

In her book, "I Thought It Was Just Me (But It Isn't): Making the Journey from 'What Will People Think?' to 'I Am Enough'" (2008), Brené Brown, renowned researcher, and bestselling author, describes shame as a "silent epidemic" that everyone experiences at some point in their life.

There are various methods of shaming, including but not limited to the following:

- Distorting the truth
- Betraying trust
- Criticizing imperfections
- Assuming the role of a victim
- Assigning blame
- Making disparaging remarks
- Imposing religious guilt
- Employing aggression
- Making unfavorable comparisons

- Criticizing one's physical appearance
- Setting unrealistic expectations
- Manipulating
- Engaging in gaslighting
- Using coded language

According to Ms. Brown, embracing vulnerability is the path to healing shame because it allows us to address the underlying emotions that contribute to feeling ashamed. When we let ourselves be vulnerable, we open the possibility of being seen and understood by others, which may help us *feel* seen and heard. By sharing our experiences and allowing ourselves to be vulnerable, we create opportunities for connection.

Vulnerability is strength disguised as weakness.

Embracing vulnerability allows us to let go of the need for perfection and control, which are often sources of shame. Instead, we embrace our imperfections and recognize that they are a natural part of being human. This kind of self-acceptance and self-compassion are crucial to the healing process.

RECLAIMING YOUR WORTH: FORGIVENESS AS SELF-CARE IN RECOVERY

Have you thought about forgiving those who have shamed you? Perhaps it seems outrageous or feels impossible, especially if the wounds are fresh, but it may be worth considering at some point.

Forgiveness doesn't mean that someone is now "off the hook" for their hurtful behavior. It doesn't require "forgetting" what they did or excusing their behavior. Instead, forgiveness is a decision you make for yourself when you're ready to *release the anger and resentment that's weighing you down.*

"You either walk inside your story and own it, or you stand outside and hustle for your worthiness." —Brené Brown

---

Ultimately, forgiveness is for **your** benefit, not theirs. Forgiveness can take place whether they ask for it or deserve it. Offering forgiveness can bring you peace and freedom from destructive anger and empower you to move forward and heal. By forgiving, you can *acknowledge your pain without letting it define you.* The person who hurt you will still face the natural consequences of their actions, but it's not your job to determine or carry them out.

If you're not ready to forgive, continue working to identify, acknowledge, and validate your feelings. This activity can be a valuable tool in discovering where you need to set some boundaries.

I recommend these two excellent TED talks by Ms. Brown:

—The Power of Vulnerability

—Listening to Shame

Chapter Sixteen
HEALING RELATIONAL TRAUMA: MOVING BEYOND VICTIMHOOD

The soul knows what to do to heal. The challenge is convincing the mind.

Many of us who've been affected by relational trauma have ugly scars and callouses on our hearts. We may have felt, or still feel, like victims, helpless and stuck. But living in a state of victimhood is damaging; it keeps us focused on our limitations and gives away our *personal power*, that wonderful sense of influence and command that we have over our own lives and circumstances.

Here's the thing: recovering from relational trauma means *reclaiming* our power, setting healthy boundaries, and making choices based on *our* needs, wants, and what is good for us mentally, spiritually, physically, socially, and emotionally.

Healing can be a beautiful and transformative journey. It requires patience, persistence, and practice, and a deep sense of self-compassion, courage, and vulnerability. And a sense of humor! The ability to laugh at ourselves is healthy; it shows that we clearly see our flaws and allow ourselves some slack. As one of my friends is fond of saying: there's no such thing as perfect.

It is wise to approach this journey without judgment, expectations, or restrictions, including the pressure of a specific time limit, because we may encounter unexpected insights along the way that call for further exploration. Each person's healing process is unique and deserves to be honored and respected.

"A friend of mine started dating someone who seemed incredibly attentive and caring at first. However, as their relationship progressed, she noticed that her partner would often make subtle jabs or criticize her in front of others, and she was constantly feeling stressed about it. This was a red flag for emotional abuse and it taught my friend the importance of recognizing her own worth and setting boundaries." —Anonymous

EMBRACING UNPREDICTABILITY AND SELF-COMPASSION

Recuperating from emotional abuse, neglect, or mistreatment requires a willingness on our part to do the work to become new and better versions of ourselves. Recovery work requires effort and making emotional investments of our time. During the process, we seek to regain our ability to trust ourselves, our memories, and others, and to make sound decisions. Forgiving *ourselves* might be an unexpected aspect of the journey as we discover how our unhealed wounds may have played a role in hurting others. It's beneficial to be kind to ourselves as we learn and grow in this process.

We wouldn't be who we are today without those painful experiences, and acknowledging their role in shaping our identity involves taking a deep dive into the past. Reframing our experiences gives us the opportunity to see those experiences anew, with a deeper understanding and to give them *new meaning*. While our painful and traumatic experiences are indeed part of our history, *they do not have to define us*.

I'm here. I'm alive. I'm grateful. I'm ready.

THE DEEP DIVE: REFRAMING PAINFUL EXPERIENCES

Thinking and feeling are distinct and separate approaches for relating to our environment, experiences, and memories. Continually thinking about our negative and hurtful encounters doesn't promote healing, and that's where many of us get stuck. Real healing requires more than educating ourselves and recalling painful memories. It takes more than adding new practices, like affirmations, meditation, or prayer. Those are *all* great for personal growth, gaining insight, and growing spiritually, and I think **it's beneficial to do any or all of those.** But in my experience, they're not enough. Here's my point: *all of those* are done on a *conscious* level. Healing emotional wounds cannot be done solely on a conscious level using cognitive processes like thinking, reasoning, and logic. While it's essential to use our cognitive abilities to learn and understand, our *emotional healing requires* us to *feel*. If we try to heal on a *conscious* level, using explanations and rationalization, we run the risk of exposing ourselves to the same kinds of pain, confusion, and frustration that we experienced when our wounds were created.

Emotional wounds: past traumas, unresolved conflicts, repressed memories, deep-seated fears, negative beliefs, and unresolved emotions like grief, anger, and shame live in the **subconscious.** It makes sense to address these wounds where they live, so it's crucial for those on this journey to feel their feelings during the healing process and beyond. Dodging the feeling process by hiding or denying the pain any time pain is felt can *intensify* your unhealed emotional hotspots. By self-avoiding, we may work hard to distract ourselves from pain by using alcohol, drugs, food, sex, shopping, gambling, or anything that suffices to keep us from hurting. Avoiding the pain of the recovery process can result in no healing, while emotional pain and triggers continue to grow. ***You can't heal if you're pretending that you haven't been hurt.***

BUILDING TRUST AND EMOTIONAL SAFETY: TO SHARE OR NOT TO SHARE?

As we heal, we must be careful when disclosing personal aspects of our relationships. Sharing our thoughts, feelings, beliefs, and ideas with anyone who is currently in an unhealthy relationship (or who hasn't recovered from their own traumatic or hurtful relationships) may spark *us* to respond inappropriately or hurtfully and potentially lead *them* to react inappropriately or hurtfully, too.

As we recover, we become better at discerning whom we can trust with our feelings and openness. We realize that only *emotionally healthy people* can *respectfully hear and accept us without their own sense of self becoming threatened.*

The people you lose during the healing process were meant to be with unhealed you.

THE JOURNEY TO SELF-VALIDATION AND INDEPENDENCE

If the idea of re-experiencing and feeling any part of your past is frightening or concerning to you, please seek help from a licensed abuse recovery expert who specializes in your specific trauma. They can provide validation, knowledge, and a sense of emotional safety. It takes courage and wisdom to seek professional help. Please don't let anything keep you from experiencing healing.

During the healing process, which is a self-focused and insightful time, we may discover that we can't control how others perceive us, and we let go of the need for their validation and approval. We protect ourselves with our boundaries and learn to detach from those who are unsuitable for us. We become comfortable allowing others to experience the naturally occurring consequences of their actions and are okay with the possibility of them disconnecting from us too.

Healing provides an opportunity for personal growth while restoring the ability to trust. Consider how healing your emotional wounds and past traumas may change your personality, goals, and relationships. How do you feel about these potential changes in yourself? You will be different. What will you be like?

Chapter Seventeen
BREAKING FREE FROM RESENTMENT

Expectations are premeditated resentments.

We all have expectations. They're the hidden rules, the "shoulds" that we set for ourselves and others, and we often don't even realize we have them until they're not met. When that happens, it can sting, leaving us hurt or resentful. So, are your expectations *really* premeditated resentments?

Let's go deeper to explore this idea further.

Resentment is the poison you drink, expecting someone else to die..

When we tie our peace or happiness to someone else's behavior, we give them the power to hurt or disappoint us. So, for our own well-being and happiness, it's essential to take a step back and take a hard look at our expectations and make changes where necessary.

Here's the thing: sometimes our expectations are unrealistic, and they can end up causing more problems than they solve. Holding onto unrealistic expectations, for ourselves and others, sets everyone up for disappointment right from the start.

It is common to associate our worth and perceived value with the expectations we hold. For instance, if I expect my friends to acknowledge my birthday and they don't, I might end up feeling unloved, forgotten, or uncared for. And if it happens, that's on me, not them. You see, my friends are unaware of my expectations because *I have not communicated them.* So, on my birthday, if I tie *their* actions to the measure of love *I feel from them,* and they don't know I've done this, is it fair to them? Is it fair to me? It is a completely no-win situation.

It is crucial to communicate your expectations openly rather than expecting others to read your mind. If I want to be remembered on my special day, I must ensure that others know my expectations, otherwise I risk feeling deeply hurt, disappointed, and resentful.

Expectations vary, ranging from high to low and realistic to unrealistic. When we have *high expectations,* meeting them can be challenging or even impossible, leading to feelings of disappointment for us or feelings of failure for the person who did not meet the expectation. On the other hand, if we tend to be people-pleasers, we may intentionally or subconsciously set *low expectations* for others to avoid disappointment for everyone involved. *Unrealistic expectations* are inflexible and do not allow for unexpected changes or flexibility, and are often rooted in fear, such as the fear of losing something or someone or the fear of someone taking something away.

Whether they are too high, too low, realistic, or not, having unfulfilled expectations often results in feeling resentful.

An expectation may look like it's fair, reasonable, and realistic, but if experience has shown that it cannot be met, we must change it. The key is to set flexible and adaptable expectations, avoiding the use of words like "never" and "always" because they lack flexibility and the possibility for change.

If you're unsure about the appropriateness of an expectation, seeking the perspective and feedback of a trusted person can be helpful. Becoming aware of your expectations and letting go of your attachment to their outcomes may reduce the chances of developing resentment in the future.

LETTING GO FOR A HAPPIER LIFE

You're aware that your interactions with others are a choice, and these interactions, along with the expectations you have, can significantly impact your relationships. For example, if you have expectations of others without understanding their current circumstances, it can lead to misunderstandings.

In my family, mind reading was a common expectation, resulting in many misunderstandings, hurt feelings, anger, and resentment. It's easy to believe that the people in our lives should "just know" what we want or need at any given moment, especially if they care about and love us.

We may *expect* them to know our needs automatically **and** we assume that they will fulfill them too! And then **we feel resentful** when they are unaware of those expectations and do not meet them. How absurd is that? And how unfair to them!

If we grow up in a dysfunctional or unhealthy environment, we may develop a mindset of expecting "bad things" to always be part of our lives. As adults this can lead us to expect the worst from others and live in fear. But changing our attitudes toward our expectations can have a profoundly positive impact on our lives. Adjusting our expectations to be more achievable may lessen our likelihood of feeling disappointed, angry, or resentful when they are unmet.

"A team member tended to overpromise and underdeliver. He made unrealistic commitments to clients without consulting the rest of us, which caused a lot of frustration and stress for us. To fix this issue, we agreed on a new process where all team members had to review and agree upon the commitments made to clients. This ensured that everyone was on the same page and that we were setting realistic expectations. It had a positive impact on our overall productivity and client satisfaction." — Anonymous

Letting go of unrealistic expectations is vital to finding peace and contentment in ourselves and our relationships. Releasing the fantasy of the "perfect" relationship is crucial to this process. Social media often perpetuates this fallacy by highlighting others' seemingly fabulous lives and relationships, provoking a fear of missing out and contributing to our feeling unhappiness and resentment. Striving for an unattainable standard will only keep us stuck and unhappy.

You don't block and delete because they won't change. You do it because **you** *have changed.*

I've learned that communicating clearly (saying what I mean and meaning what I say) can help prevent resentment from building up. A helpful tool I have discovered is to ask myself if I can take an action without feeling resentful. Now, if someone asks me to do something for them I ask myself if I can do it without feeling resentment, and if the answer is no, I politely decline without offering lengthy explanations.

As you evaluate your expectations for yourself and others, try not to judge or label your feelings.

We are constantly evolving, and by setting flexible expectations, they will grow along with us. With awareness, acceptance, and self-compassion, we can release our outdated and unrealistic expectations for ourselves and others, a significant step towards healing relational trauma.

CONSIDERATIONS FOR REDUCING RESENTMENT IN RELATIONSHIPS

- Examine an expectation you hold for someone specific. Is your expectation realistic? How do you know? How can you change it if it's not?
- How important is it that this expectation is met? Is it worth sleepless nights? Is it worth feeling anger, hurt feelings, or resentment? Is it worth losing or damaging the relationship?
- Let go of expectations around what people "should" say or do.
- Let go of outcomes. How does that feel? Scary? Anxiety-provoking? What can you do about that?
- Focus on progress, not perfection.
- Trust the process.

Chapter Eighteen
A NEW BEGINNING

Growth occurs in the quiet space between what has been and is yet to come.

FROM WOUNDS TO WISDOM: NAVIGATING THE PROCESS

Several things can happen when we experience emotional wounding in a relationship and begin doing work to heal ourselves. We may start gaining self-awareness and a deeper understanding of our feelings and emotional hotspots, and we may recognize patterns of behavior in ourselves that contributed to our emotional wounding in the first place. With self-awareness and intention, finding these patterns can help us break free to develop healthier ways of relating to others.

The healing process often involves learning to prioritize our needs and well-being. This can mean saying no to things that don't align with our values, and learning to communicate our needs and expectations clearly and assertively. These actions help create a safer and more respectful environment for us, leading to healthier and more fulfilling relationships.

As we heal past relationship wounds, we may experience a shift in perspective. We may let go of beliefs and expectations that have caused us pain and begin cultivating new ones.

Overall, healing our emotional wounds is a transformative journey in which we shift our mindset, leading to a healthier, happier life and relationships.

Happiness is not the absence of problems; it's the ability to deal with them effectively.

EMOTIONAL SCARS AND STARS: A JOURNEY OF HEALING AND GROWTH

So, let's talk about moving forward.

Here's the thing: we cannot change or control anyone's behavior. We can only change or control our own. When we fully accept this fact, it frees us to begin recovering from the confusion, trauma, scapegoating, blaming, shaming, and any other form of mistreatment we have experienced.

There is no healing without Acceptance. There is no healing without acknowledging and embracing the reality of a hurtful situation or person. There is no healing when we're hindered by judgement and resistance. Healing involves recognizing and grasping that we have no power to alter someone's thoughts or behaviors. Instead, we assume accountability *for our own thoughts, emotions, and responses.* Healing isn't about *them.* It's about *us.*

Acceptance means letting go of the desire for someone to change and freeing ourselves from the expectation that they will treat us differently or transform into a loving, kind, compassionate, and affectionate individual. We cease to resist who they are and stop investing time in wishing for them to be different. ***Our focus shifts away from them entirely.***

Do you notice the distinction? We can accept someone's true nature but are not obligated to like it. We are not required to accept unacceptable behavior; instead, we set up boundaries to safeguard ourselves.

Acceptance means relinquishing the notion that they will finally perceive us for who we are, love us unconditionally, desire to spend time with us, derive joy from our company, stop trying to change us, refrain from manipulating and hurting us, and that one day, being around them will feel safe and pleasant.

Acceptance allows us to move forward and focus on our healing and growth rather than remain consumed by the actions or behaviors of others. It is a process of surrendering and finding peace within us, even within challenging, painful circumstances and difficult relationships. It brings a sense of clarity and empowerment, allowing us to move forward and heal.

Not my circus, not my clowns.

In Acceptance, we receive all of this **on a soul level**, deeply understanding the pain we have experienced, and knowing that someone's hurtful behavior does not reflect *our* worth or value. In Acceptance, we acknowledge that the past could not have been any different. We become willing to let go of any guilt or responsibility we may have felt; we understand that we were caught up in an incomprehensible, confusing, and hurtful situation that was beyond our control.

"I knew a woman who went through a difficult divorce. She felt unable to stop dwelling on the pain, and bitterness was affecting her overall well-being. Then, with therapy, she discovered that by reframing her perspective and focusing on the lessons learned and personal growth that came out of the experience, she was able to let go of the resentment and find a sense of peace." — *Anonymous*

As we begin reframing our painful experiences with courage and self-love, we not only change our worldview, but we also fundamentally change ourselves. Instead of continuing to allow other's attitudes and behavior to define us, we see those now as only a small part of our life history. We understand that our hurtful experiences have not determined who we are, they are moments in our past that have helped to shape us. This shift in perception allows us to focus on our growth rather than linger in the pain.

Acceptance is the beginning of self-empowerment.

Once you embark on your recovery journey, you may see unexpected transformations in your thoughts, perceptions, and emotions. The order in which these changes unfold is inconsequential. You will experience healing in the areas, and at the times, which are relevant to your unique journey, following your own personal timeline.

Here are some signs that you've begun to heal. This list is by no means complete; feel free to add your own indicators, whether you've accomplished them, or they're goals for the future.

UNVEILING THE PATH: INDICATORS OF RECOVERY

- You're beginning to respect yourself.

- You've set some new boundaries.

- You focus more on what makes you happy and what's important to you rather than making others happy or knowing what's important to them.

- You've found activities you love and do them regularly.

- You're in touch with your intuition and learning to trust it.

- You realize it's not your job, and it never was, to fix anyone.

- You've examined your childhood programming, questioned each misperception you were expected to believe about yourself, and are working on letting go of someone's faulty perceptions of you.

- You're creating new ideas about who you are based on how far you've come and who you are today.

- When you see toxic behavior, you recognize it for what it is, and you steer clear.

- You're learning to fulfill your needs, and don't feel guilty about it.

- You recognize that if someone has a problem-thinking and perceiving they will probably never address it.

- You understand that your feelings were a normal reaction to abnormal behavior. Your brain was functioning precisely how it was supposed to, to protect and help you try to make sense of a situation that would never make sense.

- You're aware of when you're self-gaslighting, and you stop as soon as you become aware.

- You feel grounded and safe most of the time.

- You're getting comfortable having difficult conversations.

- You're getting comfortable confronting people who need to be confronted.

- You stand up for yourself calmly and confidently.

- You are fiercely on your own side.

- A person's character and integrity matter more to you than their popularity, sense of humor, success, or physical attributes.

- You're not interested in continuing people-pleasing behaviors.

- You like yourself.

- You're aware of your self-talk and ensure that it's positive.

- You focus more often on what makes you happy and what is important to you.

- You're continuing to develop and expand your personal values.

- You're working through your anger.

- You're working on forgiveness.

- You're learning to allow others to earn your trust.

- You notice when "red flags" are present. When avoiding those individuals is impossible, you maintain low contact and enforce your boundaries.

- You're doing recovery work regularly and acknowledging your progress.

- You believe you're a strong person.

- You're educating yourself about narcissism, toxic people, and toxic relationships.

- You're creating new beliefs about yourself based on who you've become and who you are becoming.

- You've begun to prioritize self-care in its many forms.

- You seek out and practice guided meditations that help you feel positive, strong, and peaceful.

- You journal.

- You no longer acquiesce to people or events that interrupt or intrude on your plans, privacy, safety, or serenity.

- You don't worry about whether your life choices will make someone angry or upset. You're making life choices that are all about *you* now.

- When an individual with toxic traits invites you to an argument, you decline.

- You're aware of relationships that take advantage of you.

- You focus on solutions, not problems.

- You're more concerned about your life than anyone else's.

- You no longer tolerate people who devalue or disrespect you. You remove them from your life and feel good about doing it.

- You're becoming your own advocate.

- You know what's good for you and what isn't.

- You're no longer willing to accept someone else's version of reality.

- You're unwilling to minimize your education, talents, skills, or abilities to accommodate someone else's insecurities.

- You're unwilling to minimize your education, talents, skills, or abilities to accommodate someone else's faulty perception of you.

- You know when you're being manipulated by guilt, shame, passive-aggressive behavior, and other forms of control, and you no longer let yourself be controlled.

- You're getting comfortable communicating about what you will and won't accept and do in your relationships.

- You recognize when you're being gaslighted and refuse to let your reality be rewritten by someone else.

- You'll leave situations that make you feel uncomfortable or unsafe.

- You feel worthy of being seen and heard.

- You're uncomfortable when you're in denial, and you recognize it for what it is.

- You recognize that you are a complete person and don't need validation or acceptance from anyone except yourself.

- You don't need permission to exist.

- You're no longer interested in being a people-pleaser, and you understand and accept that this kind of enabling behavior makes you a potential victim.

- You refuse to give up your plans or dreams to achieve somebody else's.

- You refuse to spend your precious time doing things you don't want to do that might gain someone's attention, affection, approval, or love.

- You've decided to stop over-functioning.

- You've decided to stop "rowing the boat" all by yourself. You understand and believe that others need to do their share of the work.

- You say "no" more often and set limits for others' behavior and expectations.

- You understand that there are consequences for every action, and you let others deal with their own consequences.

- You recognize that all relationships are two-way interactions.

- You no longer make excuses for or minimize someone's hurtful behavior.

- You don't tolerate "walking on eggshells.".

- You empathize but draw the line at being taken advantage of.

- You realize that boundaries work two ways: you no longer violate others' boundaries by rescuing or trying to fix them or their circumstances.

- You ask for clarification when confused by anything that someone says or does.

- You're getting comfortable disengaging from people with toxic traits, and you know when and why it's necessary.

- You recognize that mind games, manipulation, secrecy, intimidation, hurtful sarcasm, or teasing are toxic, and you enforce the boundaries that protect you.

- You see that praise, flattery, compliments, or charm can be subtle forms of manipulation, and those don't work on you anymore.

- You're not willing to stay in a relationship that makes you feel drained, confused, or doubtful of your sanity or your self-worth.

- You don't tolerate others crossing your personal boundaries or talking about your appearance, weight, relationships, or achievements.

- You understand that "perfection" doesn't exist and that your vulnerabilities, strengths, and weaknesses all combine to create the complete and lovable person you are.

- You accept yourself in all your imperfection.

- You trust your decision-making abilities, and you make decisions more quickly.

199 • Chapter Eighteen
A NEW BEGINNING

PART V
BUILDING HEALTHY RELATIONSHIPS

Content Warning:

This section contains frank discussions of relationship red flags, mental health challenges, and other sensitive topics including neglect and abuse. Please be aware that reading about these issues may be difficult for some readers.

Reader discretion is advised.

Chapter Nineteen
CRUCIAL ASPECTS OF A HEALTHY RELATIONSHIP

Relationships, in all their forms, are the bedrock of our lives, and they can only bring us joy, comfort, and strength if they're healthy. So, let's dive into the critical aspects of a healthy relationship.

I don't claim to be an expert or pretend to be a guru in the realm of relationships. In fact, my journey has been filled with its fair share of disastrous, traumatic, and abusive relationships! But I do believe that our past experiences, even those that were painful, can serve as steppingstones towards personal growth and a broader understanding of ourselves and others. Living through hurtful experiences has allowed me to learn some valuable life lessons about relationships, including how to cultivate healthier ones.

A healthy relationship is not just about love. It's about communication, trust, honesty, respect, equality, and security. It's about being the best version of yourself and bringing out the best in the other person. It's about growing together and building a fulfilling and meaningful connection for both of you.

LESSONS FROM THE TRENCHES: UNDERSTANDING THE PILLARS

Allow me to share the insights I've acquired from the trenches of personal experience, along with extensive reading and research, and meaningful conversations. I hope they're beneficial to you, adding a measure of confidence and wisdom to your pursuit of happier, healthier relationships.

The quality of our relationships profoundly impacts our well-being, and studies show that positive relationships contribute to longevity, enhanced stress management, healthier lifestyles, and increased immunity against common illnesses. A comprehensive review of 148 studies conducted in 2010 revealed that social connections significantly extend our life expectancy. Individuals in stable, long-term relationships have a *50% lower risk of premature death* compared to those lacking these bonds. In terms of life expectancy, the absence of healthy connections is as detrimental as smoking. (Brickel, 2017)

The profound influence of quality relationships on our overall well-being makes it crucial to understand the elements that constitute a healthy relationship. The following principles can help you develop and sustain healthy, long-lasting connections by improving the quality of your existing relationships and establishing new ones with strong foundations.

Let's dive into the key aspects of a ***healthy relationship:***

Honest and respectful communication: Things can quickly turn sour without open and respectful communication. It's not just about talking but also about listening. It entails trying to understand the other's point of view, even if you disagree. It also means expressing your emotions and thoughts openly, without the fear of being judged or facing retaliation.

Trust: Trust is the foundation of any relationship. Trust and honesty go hand in hand; having faith in someone's integrity and moral character, having confidence that they will act in your best interest. It's about being truthful, even when it may be difficult. It's also about acknowledging your mistakes and being accountable for your actions.

Respect: Respect involves recognizing and appreciating someone as a unique individual, with their own thoughts, emotions, and experiences. It means treating them with kindness and consideration, even in moments of anger or frustration. It also entails acknowledging their boundaries and prioritizing their needs.

Equality: Equality is about sharing power and control in the relationship and making decisions while respecting each other's independence. It's about giving and taking in equal measure.

Empathy: In a healthy and fulfilling relationship, empathy is crucial for building trust, emotional intimacy, and mutual understanding. It allows both individuals to feel heard, validated, and supported. Navigating conflicts, communicating effectively, and meeting each other's emotional needs becomes challenging without empathy.

Safety: A healthy relationship is marked by a sense of security and comfort. Both individuals feel safe, physically, and emotionally. You have the assurance that they will be there for you, through the ups and downs, and that you can rely on them, and they can depend on you as well.

Some key factors that contribute to *relationship longevity*, as outlined by Dr. Becker-Phelps, therapist, author, speaker, teacher (2011) are:

• Respecting each other mutually

• Engaging in activities that bring mutual joy and happiness

• Prioritizing shared time

• Valuing and cherishing the time spent together

• Practicing the art of giving and receiving

• Keeping a solid commitment to each other, even during periods of conflict or disinterest

• Fostering effective communication

• Learning and using problem-solving skills

• Committing to resolve conflicts and disagreements in a respectful manner

• Being open to forgiving and accepting forgiveness

• Setting up and agreeing upon realistic expectations and showing a willingness to fulfill them

• Having shared values, priorities, and attitudes about family, friends, and parenting (if applicable)

• Cultivating a satisfying and fulfilling sexual relationship (if applicable)

Recognizing a healthy relationship can be challenging, especially if you have experienced unhealthy ones in the past. Here are *some signs to look for in yourself:*

- You feel happy and content most of the time.
- You can express your thoughts and feelings freely.
- You feel heard and understood.
- You trust and feel trusted in return.
- You feel respected and valued.
- You feel safe and secure.
- You can be yourself without fear of judgment or rejection.

No relationship is perfect. There will always be ups and downs, disagreements, and misunderstandings. However, in a healthy relationship, these are dealt with *through open communication, mutual respect, and a willingness to negotiate and compromise* so both of you feel fairly treated. The key is not just knowing these principles but practicing them every day.

A JOURNEY TOWARDS LOVE: CULTIVATING NEW RELATIONSHIPS

Meeting someone with whom you can have a healthy relationship is a journey that requires self-awareness, patience, and a clear understanding of what you want in a partner. Here are some things to consider:

- **Know Yourself:** Before you can find a partner who complements you, you must first understand yourself. What are your values, passions, and goals? What do you need in a relationship? What do you need from a partner? Understanding these core aspects of yourself is vital to find potential partners who align with your life and values.
- **Set Healthy Boundaries:** Healthy relationships are built on understanding and respecting each other's boundaries.
- **Look for Emotional Maturity:** Emotional maturity is vital to a healthy relationship. This includes the ability to express emotions in a healthy way, empathize with others, and handle conflict constructively.
- **Shared Interests and Values:** While opposites may attract, having shared interests and values supplies a

solid foundation for a relationship. Consider those who share your passions or at least respect them.

- **Communication Skills:** Communication is the lifeblood of any relationship. Look for someone willing to communicate openly, honestly, and respectfully.
- **Patience:** Finding the right person can take time. Please don't rush into a relationship out of fear of being alone. It's better to wait for a relationship that is healthy and fulfilling.

Remember, no one is perfect, and every relationship has challenges. But knowing what you want and need, setting and respecting your boundaries, and being patient can increase your chances of finding someone compatible with your values and aspirations, and developing a fulfilling relationship.

NURTURING THE BONDS: MAINTAINING HEALTHY RELATIONSHIPS

Building and keeping strong and healthy relationships can sometimes take unexpected turns, leaving us confused or unsure of how to fix issues that arise. Often, we unknowingly avoid confronting them until it becomes challenging to understand what went wrong and figure out how to fix it. So, it is crucial to face relationship problems directly to assess their impact and find solutions. It can feel like navigating a labyrinth, unsure of the next move, and sometimes, we may find ourselves at a dead-end, feeling confused and uncertain about how to proceed. Often, these unexpected developments result from unresolved problems that have been avoided or ignored. We may avoid facing the issues due to our fear of conflict, or simply because we don't know how to approach them. But avoidance only compounds the problem. Left unaddressed, any problem can fester and grow, leading to misunderstandings, resentment, and communication breakdowns, in effect, making it worse.

Understanding what went wrong can be challenging and requires a willingness to critically look at our own actions and behaviors and to *accept our part* in the situation. It requires a willingness on our part to admit fault or responsibility. It also involves open, honest, and respectful communication, which can be difficult when emotions run high. It can become a process of untangling a web of difficulties that have been ignored or avoided by naming and acknowledging them and understanding their root causes, taking steps to address them. This could mean engaging in difficult and uncomfortable conversations, changing our behavior, and seeking professional help.

It's okay to feel confused or unsure and not have all the answers. What's important is the willingness to face concerns head-on and commit to working towards a resolution. Facing challenges together allows us to grow and strengthen our connection.

KNOWING WHEN TO HOLD ON OR LET GO

Can a relationship marked by red flags be salvaged? Well, there's no straightforward answer.

Red flags are indicators of potential problems, issues, or danger, however, not all red flags are equal and should not be treated as such. For example, red flags that suggest emotional unavailability or potential abuse are serious and should be addressed at once. Experts advise that if a person shows signs of abusive behavior, whether physical or emotional, it's recommended to leave that relationship because of the potential danger involved.

Go where your energy is celebrated, appreciated, and reciprocated.

On the other hand, if the red flag is less severe, it might be worth discussing to see if it's an issue that can be resolved together. Our current culture often encourages people to abandon relationships at the first sign of discomfort or to obsess over minor traits based on personal preferences when it might be more beneficial to *understand the reasoning* behind the choice. This approach promotes open communication and problem-solving, critical components of a healthy relationship. For example, it's not necessarily a red flag if someone has no social media presence, but it is unusual, and you would certainly want to learn more about that choice.

MOVING FORWARD: EMBRACING THE CHALLENGES

Navigating the twists and turns of life together is a testament to our commitment to each other in any relationship. It is through shared experiences that we deepen our connections and create lasting memories. Whether it's celebrating triumphs or supporting each other during difficult times, our commitment to embracing life's ups and downs fosters a sense of unity.

"A close friend of mine was in an abusive relationship where physical violence was a regular occurrence. He would use physical force to assert dominance and control, leaving my friend with visible injuries and emotional scars. It was a terrifying situation that required intervention and support to help her escape." —Anonymous

We know that building and keeping any relationship requires effort and commitment, and the rewards that come can be immeasurable. When we prioritize the ***essential elements*** of a healthy relationship, such as effective communication, mutual respect, and shared values, we lay the foundation for love, trust, and growth.

In our journey to protect or rescue ourselves from the effects of ill-treatment by others and begin cultivating more enjoyable relationships, we must embrace the challenges that will inevitably show up. These potential difficulties will provide us with opportunities for personal and relational growth by allowing us to learn and evolve. We can create a solid framework that allows love, trust, and growth to flourish. It is through our dedication and willingness to put in the *effort* that we build fulfilling relationships.

Knowledge is power. By arming ourselves with an understanding of relationship red flags, we can consciously avoid potentially harmful individuals with confidence, and devote our efforts towards cultivating nurturing relationships. I hope you embrace this journey of self-discovery and growth, and may it lead to relationships that bring you joy, fulfillment, and lasting happiness.

GLOSSARY OF TERMS

Algorithm: algorithms are complex mathematical formulas social media platforms use to determine what content to show users. These algorithms analyze user preferences, engagement levels, and relevance to decide which posts, ads, or recommendations will most likely interest each user. These algorithms aim to enhance user experience by showing them content they are more likely to engage with, thereby increasing user satisfaction and platform use.

Boundaries: protect us from someone else's behavior or from engaging in activities that we'd rather not. Setting healthy boundaries protects and empowers us about our safety, emotional stability, and mental health.

Codependent (enabler): an individual with an emotional and behavioral illness affecting their ability to have healthy, mutually satisfying relationships. Codependency is a learned behavior, so it's passed down through generations. It occurs when a person supports or enables another person's addiction, mental health challenges, immaturity, irresponsibility, or underachievement. Codependents rely on others for identity, approval, or affirmation. They are "people-pleasers" who willingly play by the "rules" of others, losing their identity in the process.

Cognitive dissonance: the mental discomfort experienced from holding two or more contradictory beliefs, ideas, or values. It results from grappling with discrepancies between what you believe to be true and **what you are**

told to believe is true. It's that surreal moment when you **know** that you heard or saw X, but you're told that you saw Y. You know what you saw but you still question it because you doubt your senses and your ability to remember accurately.

Cognitive empathy: having the *intellectual* understanding that someone is feeling a particular emotion but not feeling anything in response to that awareness.

Complex Post-Traumatic Stress Disorder (C-PTSD): results from a series of trauma-causing events or one prolonged event, while PTSD is usually related to a single traumatic event. Complex Post-Traumatic Stress Disorder can be a result of narcissistic abuse. Common symptoms include flashbacks, panic attacks, nightmares, overactive startle response, and habitually thinking about the traumatic event.

Diagnostic and Statistical Manual (DSM): a publication by the American Psychiatric Association used by clinicians to classify and diagnose mental disorders in children and adults. There have been several iterations of the DSM, the most recent of which was completed in 2013 and known as the fifth edition or DSM-5 (DSM-V).

Dissociation: losing the sense of "who I am, where I am, or what I'm doing." It's a protective response that allows emotional separation from trauma or abuse as it's happening.

Ego: the part of the mind that arbitrates between the conscious and the subconscious. It's responsible for our sense of self (personal identity) and is the filter through which we see ourselves. We tell our ego-specific "stories" to continue living with certain self-defining beliefs.

Emotional empathy: the ability to put ourselves in another person's place and feel their emotions.

Empathy gene: referred to in a study published March 12, 2018, in the journal *Translational Psychiatry*, and the most extensive genetic study of empathy to date. It found that "how empathetic" we are partly due to genetics. — University of Cambridge.

Enabling: taking responsibility, blaming, or making excuses for a person's harmful or hurtful behavior. Also known as Codependency.

Gaslight: a tactic used to gain power and control over an individual by prompting them to doubt their senses or memory. Gaslighting is a form of emotional manipulation in which a person or group causes someone to question their own sanity, perception, or memories. It involves the abuser denying or distorting the truth, making the victim doubt their reality, and often leads to the victim feeling confused, anxious, and powerless. Gaslighting is a harmful tactic used by manipulative individuals to gain control and power over others by causing them to question their reality and doubt their memory and judgment.

Love Bombing: A manipulative tactic to gain control and power over someone. It involves showering the other person with excessive affection, attention, and compliments to create an intense and overwhelming emotional bond. This tactic is often seen in the early stages of a relationship, where the love-bomber may appear to be the perfect partner, constantly doting and making grand gestures of affection.

Love-bombing can be incredibly deceptive and emotionally damaging. Excessive attention and affection can make the recipient feel incredibly special and desired, but it's important to know that this behavior is not genuine or sustainable. The love-bomber is not genuinely interested in the well-being or happiness of the other; instead, they use these tactics to control them.

Mixed message: a type of communication where an individual gives conflicting information, either verbal or non-verbal.

Narcissistic injury: anything a narcissist perceives as a threat to their 'false self' or their sense of importance and dominance.

Narcissistic Personality Disorder (NPD): a recognized mental disorder listed in the Diagnostic and Statistical Manual of Mental Disorders. It falls under the category of Personality Disorders and is characterized by nine specific criteria. To receive a diagnosis of NPD, an individual must show at least five of these criteria:

1. grandiose sense of self-importance

2. preoccupied with fantasies of unlimited success, power, beauty, etc.

3. believes they are "special" and can only be understood by or associated with like-minded people

4. requires excessive admiration

5. feels entitled to and expects special treatment

6. manipulative and exploitative

7. lacks empathy

8. envious of others and believes others are envious of them

9. arrogant or haughty behavior.

Narcissistic rage: intense anger, aggression, or passive-aggression displayed by a narcissist when they experience a setback or challenges their illusion of grandiosity, entitlement, or superiority, triggering their inadequacy, shame, and vulnerability. –Psychology Today, July 8, 2018

Narcissistic supply (NS): a concept introduced by Otto Fenichel in 1938, describing a type of admiration and support that a narcissist takes from their environment. It is essential to their self-esteem.

No contact (NC): an example of a boundary used to prevent recurring abuse. It is usually considered to be a "last resort" for protection against dysfunctional or abusive behavior.

Passive-aggression: involves showing aggression in a passive, more socially acceptable way.

Personal Power: refers to an individual's sense of control and influence over their life and circumstances. It is closely related to self-efficacy, which is the belief in one's ability to achieve specific goals. Personal power includes confidence, assertiveness, and the ability to make decisions and act. It is an essential aspect of worth because when individuals feel a sense of personal power, they are more likely to believe in their abilities and take proactive measures toward achieving their goals.

Post Traumatic Stress Disorder: a mental health challenge caused by exposure to an incredibly stressful event like a natural disaster, accident, assault, terrorist event, war, loss of a loved one, receiving an illness diagnosis, and hospitalization.

Projection: attributing a trait we dislike in ourselves onto someone else.

Reaction: a reciprocal or counteracting force, typically quick, without much thought. Aggressive.

Response: a thoughtful, calm, and non-threatening reply.

Scapegoating: a practice seen in dysfunctional families. The scapegoat is the person who gets blamed for offenses and injustices that happen to family members, and the role can be temporary or permanent. Family members other than the narcissistic parent take turns in the scapegoat role. The narcissistic parent decides the scapegoat.

Self-avoid: behavior that helps avoid or escape particular thoughts or feelings. It can involve "doing" or "not doing" something. –Psychology Today, March 5, 2013

Self-gaslighting: a form of self-doubt and self-deception that contributes to maintaining codependency. It's a consequence of accepting continual blame or living in a dysfunctional environment with inadequate emotional support.

Silent treatment: a way to inflict pain without causing visible marks. Research shows that "ignoring" or "excluding" someone activates the part of the brain where physical pain is experienced.

Trauma bond: powerful emotional bonds that are created between two individuals undergoing cycles of abuse together. Over time, trauma bonds become very resistant to change, and a codependent relationship develops.

Triangulation: a key sign of toxicity, first mentioned in chapter two, is the manipulation of a relationship between two people by a third person controlling the amount and type of communication between them. It generates rivalry between the two parties to "divide and conquer."

Triggering: reacting to old, buried memories with an automatic, unconscious behavior. Triggers indicate the presence of unhealed wounds.

Validation: the act of recognizing or affirming someone's feelings or thoughts as sound or worthwhile. Validation is essential to parenting because it contributes to effective and safe communication. Feeling heard and understood leads to feelings of trust, a cornerstone of every relationship.

Virtue signaling: the not-so-humble announcement of one's character traits, moral views, or values.

REFERENCES

Alzheimer's Disease fact Sheet. (n.d.). National Institute on Aging.
https://www.nia.nih.gov/health/alzheimers-disease-fact-sheet#

American Psychiatric Association. Alternative DSM-5 *model for personality disorders*. Fifth Edition. Washington, DC: American Psychiatric Publishing, Inc; 2013. 761-81.

American Psychiatric Association, 2013. *Diagnostic and Statistical Manual of Mental Disorders, 5th Edition*. American Psychiatric Association Publishing, Arlington, VA.

American Psychiatric Association (n.d.). *Warning Signs of Mental Illness*. Psychiatry.org.
https://www.psychiatry.org/patients-families/warning-signs-of-mental-illness

Baskin-Sommers, A., Krusemark, E., & Ronningstam, E. (2014, July). *Empathy in Narcissistic Personality Disorder: from clinical and empirical perspectives.* Retrieved July 10, 2019, from
https://www.ncbi.nlm.nih.gov/pmc/articles/PMC4415495/

Booz, A. N. (2023, June 14). *30 physical signs of Intuition: When to trust your gut.* GenTwenty.

https://gentwenty.com/physical-signs-of-intuition/

Bouchez, C. (2005, December 31). 10 Signs of an Ailing Mind. WebMD. https://www.webmd.com/mental-health/features/10-signs-ailing-mind

Boyes, A. (2013, January 17). 50 *Common Cognitive Distortions*. Retrieved August 2, 2019, from https://www.psychologytoday.com/us/blog/in-practice/201301/50-common-cognitive-distortions.

Bressert, S. (2019, March 19). *Dependent personality disorder symptoms*. Retrieved July 7, 2019, from https://psychcentral.com/disorders/dependent-personality-disorder/symptoms/.

Brickel, Robyn E. M. A. (2017, September 11). Healthy relationships matter more than we think. PsychAlive. https://www.psychalive.org/healthy-relationships-matter/

Brown, Brené. (2008). I thought it was just me (but it isn't): making the journey from "what will people think" to "I am enough." New York: Gotham Books.

Drescher, A., on, U., 29, A., & (Hons), A. D. H. W. (2023). Retrieved from https://www.simplypsychology.org/narcissist-gaslighting.html

Duignan, B. (n.d.). *What's the difference between a psychopath and a sociopath? And how do both differ from narcissists?* Retrieved December 21, 2019, from https://www.britannica.com/story/whats-the-difference-between-a-psychopath-and-a-sociopath-and-how-do-both-differ-from-narcissists.

Dumain, T. (2022). Retrieved from https://www.webmd.com/mental-health/addiction/substance-abuse

Eddy, W. A. (2018). 5 Types of people who can ruin your life: Identifying and dealing with narcissists, sociopaths, and other high-conflict personalities. New York: TarcherPerigee.

Franco, F. (2018, March 19). *Attachment and C-PTSD: How complex trauma gets in the way*. Retrieved July 28, 2019, from https://www.goodtherapy.org/blog/attachment-and-c-ptsd-how-complex-trauma-gets-in-the-way-0322185.

Gattuso, R. (2018, March 28). Complex PTSD: How a new diagnosis differs from standard PTSD. Retrieved December 20, 2019, from https://www.talkspace.com/blog/complex-ptsd-versus-standard-ptsd/

Goleman, D. (2010). *Emotional intelligence*. London: Bloomsbury.

Gould, W. R. (2023). Retrieved from https://www.verywellmind.com/10-red-flags-in-relationships-5194592

Hammond, C. (2018, November 10). *The Narcissistic Cycle of Abuse*. Retrieved November 10, 2019, from https://pro.psychcentral.com/exhausted-woman/2015/05/the-narcissistic-cycle-of-abuse/.

Hammond, C. (2018, Oct 7). What is narcissism awareness grief (NAG)? Retrieved August 2, 2019, from https://growwithchristine.com/what-is-narcissism-awareness-grief-nag/

Hodges, S. D., & Myers, Michael W. (2007). Empathy. In R. F. Baumeister and K. D. Vohs (Eds.), *Encyclopedia of social psychology* (pp. 296-298). Thousand Oaks, CA: Sage.

Holmes, L. (2018). Retrieved from https://www.huffpost.com/entry/signs-of-an-eating-disorder

Hudson, M. (2023). The road to recovery: Finding the best therapy for narcissistic personality disorder. Counseling Solutions of Texas. https://www.counselingsolutionstexas.com/blog-post/the-road-to-recovery-finding-the-best-therapy-for-narcissistic-personality-disorder

Keohan, LCSW, E. (2023, June 22). Therapy for narcissistic personality disorder - talkspace. Mental Health Conditions. https://www.talkspace.com/mental-health/conditions/narcissistic-personality-disorder/therapy-treatment-types/

Loryngalardi. (2021, January 15). Don't ignore your gut feelings. Loryn Galardi.

https://www.loryngalardi.com/post/don-t-ignore-your-gut-feelings/

McBride, K. (2018, February 19). *The real effect of narcissistic parenting on children.* Retrieved October 3, 2019, from https://www.psychologytoday.com/us/blog/the-legacy-distorted-love/201802/the-real-effect-narcissistic-parenting-children.

National Alliance on Mental Illness (n.d.). Nami.org. https://www.nami.org/About-Mental-Illness/Warning-Signs-and-Symptoms

National Institute on Alcohol Abuse and Alcoholism: "Rethinking Drinking: Alcohol and Your Health."

Phelps, L.-B. (2011). 10 benefits of happy relationships https://drbecker-phelps.com/webmd_p40/

Ronningstam EF, Maltsberger JT. Part X: Personality Disorders. *Gabbard GO. Gabbard's Treatments of Psychiatric Disorders.* Fourth Edition. Washington DC: American Psychiatric Publishing; 2007. Chapter 52: Narcissistic Personality Disorder, pages 791-804.

Saeed, K. (2019, August 5). *How to deal with the silent treatment and gain the upper hand.* Retrieved December22, 2019, https://kimsaeed.com/2019/07/28/how-to-deal-with-the-silent-treatment-and-gain-the-upper-hand/.

Tanasugarn, A. (2022). Retrieved from https://www.psychologytoday.com/us/blog/understanding-ptsd/202206/4-common-patterns-coercive-control-in-relationships

Walker, L. E. (2017). *The battered woman syndrome*. New York: Springer Publishing Company.

Warrior, E. (2023, April 13). *Toxic people making you feel off gut feeling*. Medium. https://medium.com/@empathicwarrior/toxic-people-making-you-feel-off-gut-feeling-109bcb87c3ce

Warrier, V., Toro, R., Chakrabarti, B., Børglum, A. D., Grove, J., Hinds, D. A., Baron Cohen, S. (2018). Retrieved from https://www.nature.com/articles/s41398-017-0082-6

WebMD. (2022, December 18). Toxic person: Signs to look for. WebMD. https://www.webmd.com/mental-health/signs-toxic-person#091e9c5e82092525-1-2

BIBLIOGRAPHY

Atkinson, Angela (2015). *Take back your life: 103 highly effective strategies to snuff out a narcissist's gaslighting and enjoy the happy life you really deserve.*

Greenberg, E. (2016). Borderline, narcissistic, and schizoid adaptations: The pursuit of love, admiration, and safety. New York, NY: Greenbrooke Press.

Hartney, E. (2019, May 12). Do You Know About Dissociation? Retrieved August 5, 2019, from https://www.verywellmind.com/what-is-dissociation-22201.

Krause-Utz, A., Frost, R., Winter, D., & Elzinga, B. M. (2017). Dissociation and Alterations in Brain Function and Structure: Implications for Borderline Personality Disorder. *Current Psychiatry Reports*, 19(1). doi: 10.1007/s11920-017-0757-y

Lanius, R.A., Vermetten, E., Loewenstein, R. J., Brand, B., Schmahl, C., Bremner, J. D., & Spiegel, D. (2010). Emotion modulation in PTSD: Clinical and neurobiological evidence for a dissociative subtype. *American Journal of Psychiatry*, 167(6), 640–647. doi:10.1176/appi.ajp. 2009.09081168)

National Institute on Drug Abuse: "The Science of Drug Abuse and Addiction: The Basics," "Easy to Read Drug Facts," "Drugs, Brains, and Behavior: The Science of

Addiction," "Synthetic Cathinones ("Bath Salts")," "Cocaine," "Heroin," "MDMA (Ecstasy, Molly)," "Prescription and Over-the-Counter (OTC) Medicine," "Health Consequences of Drug Misuse."

Schwartz, A. (2019, December 17). *Complex PTSD and attachment trauma.* Retrieved July 20, 2019, https://drarielleschwartz.com/complex-ptsd-and-attachment-trauma-dr-arielle-schwartz/.

Sederer, Lloyd I. (2009). *Blueprints Psychiatry* (Fifth ed.). Philadelphia: Wolters Kluwer/Lippincott Williams & Wilkins. p. 29. ISBN 9780781782531. Archived from the original on 11 January 2017 – via Google Books.

Skodol, A. E., Bender, D. S., & Morey, L. C. (2014). Narcissistic personality disorder in DSM-5. *Personality Disorders: Theory, Research, and Treatment*, 5(4), 422–427. doi: 10.1037/per0000023

Stines, S. (2019, July 8). *Narcissist's Mixed Messages.* Retrieved June 15, 2019, from https://pro.psychcentral.com/recovery-expert/2019/04/narcissists-mixed-messages/.

Subby, R. (1987). *Lost in the shuffle the co-dependent reality.* Health Communications.

Toll, A. (2013). *Be honest with me: an exploration of lies in relationships.* Retrieved Jan 10, 2019, from

https://dc.uwm.edu/cgi/viewcontent.cgi?article=1168&cont
ext=etd.

Vaknin, S. (2008, November 27). *The Inverted Narcissist*.
Retrieved on 2023, September 25 from
https://www.healthyplace.com/personality-
disorders/malignant-self-love/the-inverted-narcissist_.

Weinheimer, J., Russo, J., Giblock, D., & Kuber, J. (2020,
January 27). *NPD statistics*. Retrieved January 30, 2020,
from https://www.therecoveryvillage.com/mental-
health/narcissistic-personality-disorder/related/npd-
statistics_.

Wingenfeld, K., & Wolf, O. T. (2014). *Stress, memory, and
the hippocampus*. Retrieved November 12, 2018, from
https://www.ncbi.nlm.nih.gov/pubmed/24777135_.

Zweig, Connie (1991). *Meeting the Shadow*. Los Angeles:
J.P. Tarcher. ISBN 0-87477-618-X. p. 24.

ACKNOWLEDGMENTS

I am profoundly grateful to those whose tireless efforts and unwavering encouragement played a role in bringing this book to completion.

To my dear husband Kim, and my much-loved children Christin and Matthew, your support has been my anchor throughout this journey. You rock!

A special note of gratitude goes to my proofreaders, Marlene Gross-Ackeret, Gayle Shinder, Diane Askwyth, and Rev. Hollie Ann Brooks, LMHC. These remarkable women generously devoted their time to meticulously proofread, edit, and offer insightful feedback and suggestions. Your honesty and commitment to the task are deeply appreciated. I am forever grateful for your contributions.

Lastly, I want to express my thankfulness to all my subscribers who sent in personal red flag stories. You know who you are. Your willingness to share these phenomenal experiences is truly appreciated!

ABOUT THE AUTHOR

Diane Metcalf is an experienced advocate, speaker, and author specializing in abuse and family dynamics.

She holds a Bachelor of Arts degree in Psychology and a Master of Science in Information Technology. Her professional portfolio is diverse, encompassing fields such as Domestic and Partner Abuse Counseling, Geriatric Care Management, Developmental Disability Services, Vocational Rehabilitation, Information Technology Management, and Education.

She is the author of the highly praised "Lemon Moms" series, an emotionally supportive collection that dives into the effects of growing up with mothers having narcissistic traits. This compassionate trilogy provides valuable insights and guidance for coming to terms with past traumas to initiate the healing process.

Through her personal journey and experiences with emotional abuse, and her ongoing work in healing and self-improvement, she has developed effective strategies to recover and move forward from abusive, neglectful, and non-nurturing relationships. She happily shares these with others seeking growth in their own recovery.

Diane's writings, which focus on healing relational trauma through awareness, intention, and introspection, combined with healthy coping processes and tools, can be found on "The Toolbox" at toolbox.dianemetcalf.com.

She shares her home in Nevada with her husband and cherished pets.

This book is intended for informational purposes and is not a substitute for professional therapy.

WHAT'S NEXT?

Learn more about recovering from hurtful, toxic, and non-nurturing relationships!

Find my latest **books, freebies and offers** on DianeMetcalf.com

Sign up for free tools and strategies:

The Toolbox: toolbox.dianemetcalf.com

Your *Free Gift*:

An Inner Child Guided Healing Meditation MP3

BOOKS BY DIANE METCALF

1. **Lemon Moms: A Guide to Understand and Survive Maternal Narcissism** Why you can't please her, why she withholds love and affection, and why nothing you do is ever good enough.

2. **Lemon Moms Companion Workbook:** Action Steps to Understand and Survive Maternal Narcissism

3. **Lemon Moms Life-Altering Affirmations, Change Your Self-talk, Change YourSELF-** 200+ pre-written affirmations to help you move forward from the effects of toxic relationships. Addresses gaslighting, neglect, deceit, trauma bonding, shaming, and other forms of emotional mistreatment.

4. **I AM: A Guided Journey to Your Authentic Self, Workbook and Journal-** learn how to write powerful affirmations to help you manifest love, positivity, peace, self-confidence, motivation, success, and other wonderful things.

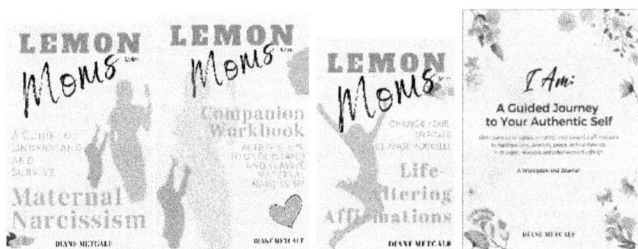

Available on Amazon and wherever books are sold.

LOVE THIS BOOK?

Don't forget to leave a review!

Your review helps others find this book, and it helps make future versions better!

Head to Amazon (or wherever you bought this book) to let us know your thoughts.

Thank you so much. I appreciate you!

Get Free Shipping on My Books: DianeMetcalf.com